MW01622700

“When I saw my Unique Ability Statement, it was very emotional. I vibrated. It’s like when somebody tells the truth and says, ‘I know you.’ It was like after all these years, I discovered myself.”

Jean-Pierre Blanchet

“When you’re in your Unique Ability zone for extended periods of time, you can get a lot done, and it’s not draining. It’s almost effortless.”

Scott Cohen

“Being clear on my Unique Ability has validated what I had thought were my talents. This validation has boosted my confidence to go out to the world and grow my business more.”

Oabona Kgengwenyane

“It’s a pole star thing. Knowing what my Unique Ability is keeps me from getting lost and reminds me how to be my best Hamish.”

Hamish MacDonald

“It makes me very confident about what I should be focusing my energy on—and what I shouldn’t. I don’t feel guilty about not being good in certain areas. I’m more accepting of myself, less hard on myself.”

Myrna Nemirsky

Printed in Toronto, Canada. April 2018. The Strategic Coach Inc., 33 Fraser Avenue, Suite 201, Toronto, Ontario, M6K 3J9.

This publication is meant to strengthen your common sense, not to substitute for it. It is also not a substitute for the advice of your doctor, lawyer, accountant, or any of your advisors, personal or professional.

Library and Archives Canada Cataloguing in Publication

Nomura, Catherine, 1967-, author
Unique ability 2.0 discovery : define your best self / Catherine Nomura, Julia Waller, Shannon Waller.

Previous title: Unique ability : creating the life you want.
ISBN 978-1-897239-41-4 (paperback)

1. Self-actualization (Psychology). 2. Ability. I. Waller, Julia, 1966-, author II. Waller, Shannon, 1965-, author III. Title. IV. Title: Unique ability.

BF637.S4N652 2015 158.1 C2015-904768-4

Preface

It started with a few stories. We sat down to update the book *Unique Ability: Creating The Life You Want* on the eve of its tenth anniversary and thought we'd gather a few updated stories for the second edition. And then the onslaught began.

The more people we spoke to who had recently been through The Unique Ability Discovery Process with Julia Waller, our in-house Unique Ability coach, the more it became clear that something had shifted. The results they were getting were significantly more profound than they had been when our first book was written. Person after person attributed this to Julia's great coaching, to how she had coaxed and prodded and inspired them to dig deeper and really uncover the heart of who they are in all areas of their lives. We realized that we wanted to include the coaching that Julia developed over the ten years since the original book in our updated version.

If you're one of many who read the original book or were introduced to the Process early on, what you'll find here is a comprehensive guide, with new wisdom on how to get to the core of what you love to do and do best more quickly, and how to express it more profoundly. We've made it the first in a series, focusing this volume and its accompanying Notebook on how to discover your Unique Ability.

If this is your first exposure to the concept of Unique Ability, read on knowing that the thinking and exercises you're about to go through have been honed and tested through 25 years of working on Unique Ability with thousands of Strategic Coach entrepreneurial clients, their teams, kids and spouses, and through Julia's intensive one-on-one sessions with hundreds of people.

The benefits of understanding your Unique Ability can't be overstated. It's a depth of self-knowledge that allows you to live more consciously in a way that creates the most joy and growth for you and the most value for others—to have the clarity, sense of "permission," and freedom to create and live the life you truly want. And it all starts with doing the work in this book. I know I speak for my co-authors and everyone at Strategic Coach in saying we're thrilled to be able to help you along on this journey!

Catherine Nomura
July 2015

Acknowledgements

This book is truly the result of Unique Ability® Teamwork in action. We would like to thank, first and foremost, Dan Sullivan and Babs Smith for creating the concept of Unique Ability® and articulating it so that so many others could benefit. None of this would exist without their commitment to first living this way themselves and then creating Strategic Coach, the company and the Program. This has given our team a remarkable Unique Ability-centered environment in which to learn, grow, and be appreciated. It's also provided our clients with tools and a structure in which to develop their own Unique Abilities, while simplifying their lives and growing their businesses exponentially.

We're also incredibly grateful for the many Strategic Coach® clients, their family members, and our team members who shared their Unique Ability stories so we could share them with you. Their experiences, insights, and testimonials bring authenticity to this book and provide inspiration and ideas that the concepts and exercises alone could never convey. The many people we interviewed, who each shared so generously, continue to amaze us with their extraordinary talents and how, coupled with remarkable passion and drive, they use these to create good in the world. Many thanks also to the readers whose "outside eyes" helped us make some critical refinements that we were too deep in the project to see.

The ease of use of this book and Notebook owe much to our incredibly talented, collaborative, and industrious design and production team, who were absolutely instrumental in helping us make a massive amount of information navigable, digestible, and beautiful to look at. A special thanks to Suzanne Noga, our lead designer, for her tireless work in developing an engaging yet practical design, and for continually innovating new design solutions; to Kory Simpson, our project manager, for keeping us all on course; to Myrna Nemirsky for her always meticulous editing and proofreading skills that make us all look better; to Jen Bhatthal for patiently making endless text and layout changes; to Kerri Morrison for bravely being the final "check" before printing; and to Christine Nishino for shepherding this through the production and printing process to a beautiful physical product we're all proud of.

And last, thanks to you for having the courage to see a bigger future for yourself and take action to make it a reality. People like you are why we do what we do.

To Babs and Dan, for showing us the possibility of a Unique Ability-centered life.

Unique Ability®
2.0

contents

Unique Ability®
2.0

Foreword by Dan Sullivan

I've often said that my discovery of the notion that Unique Ability is something everyone has, first came as a result of a report I was hired to design and write by a Canadian Member of Parliament back in 1980. Part of my job was to go across the country and interview people with disabilities. In the course of this, it became clear that the most successful of those I met had learned how to focus on and leverage their unique strengths. In other words, they'd built their lives around their abilities, not their disabilities. During these interviews, it dawned on me that we all have disabilities, areas in which we're not so capable, and also areas of ability where we have the possibility of achieving extraordinary results. It's by strengthening the latter that we each have the greatest opportunity for success, and the freedom to determine our most satisfying path in life.

Recently, after more than 30 years of coaching and thinking about Unique Ability, I realized that the seeds of this insight were actually with me since childhood. I knew very early on that if I just focused on things I really liked and did really well, there was no need to pay much attention to how other people did things to know how to be in the world. The basis for expansion was inside of me.

I was lucky enough to grow up in circumstances that allowed me a lot of freedom to explore this. For instance, as a child, I created my own education system. I would start with an article in the *Encyclopedia Britannica* about something interesting and then follow the cross-references through other related topics to create my own learning journey. My mother let me skip school to go to the library and do this. To this day, I enjoy reading multiple online publications and a wide range of books, and integrating the most interesting insights and tidbits into a larger context for understanding the world. This context forms the basis for what I provide to my clients, who are some of the world's most successful entrepreneurs.

Looking back now, I can see that I was always educating myself based on what I was really interested in. Right from the beginning, somehow, I naturally took this self-organizing approach, which even then was quite unusual. It was an instinct, but until I really recognized its value, it was still possible to get off track. I'd find myself in situations where I could get bogged down by obligations or commitments to activities that didn't inspire that same fascination and didn't create great results—activities that were not in alignment with my Unique Ability.

Conditions in the world have changed a lot since I was in first grade in the 1950s. Back then, there was a belief that if you followed the education system's template, not only would you do well in school, you'd actually fit in well out in the marketplace. The impetus then was not to look inside oneself, but to trust others to provide a path for your success.

I think the predictability in the conventional educational model has gone away. Today, it's challenging to find work even after graduating from college. You've got bright people with respected degrees from respected universities either not finding employment or settling for jobs that have nothing to do with their education, just to get paid. This is because technology renders things obsolete so quickly in today's world that much of what you learn is out of date before you even graduate. From the point of view of the individual, technology penalizes a curriculum's tendency to be predictable and repetitive. Instead, it puts a premium on unique behavior and innovation.

This is why focusing on one's Unique Ability—that unique superior skill combined with passion that every individual possesses—is so much more important to success and happiness for everyone today than it was even 30 years ago. It's a tremendous advantage economically, psychologically, and from an evolutionary standpoint. I see it so clearly in my own experience, and in the experience of over 16,000 entrepreneurs that we've coached at Strategic Coach over the past 25 years. From the perspective of your Unique Ability, no matter what it is, the future is full of opportunity, and there's a simplicity because you're very clear about what's on the right path and what's not. You don't need to spend a lot of energy guessing about who or what you should be, or wondering if a particular opportunity or choice is right for you. When it's your path, you create it as you go with Unique Ability as your guide, and its constant evolution becomes your life's work and enjoyment.

Your Unique Ability is the natural core of your own personalized, self-organizing, real-time lifetime school. It's the way to create your own ever-evolving, cutting-edge template for value creation, using your own interests and what creates the most value for others as a guide, and your obstacles and experiences as lessons and growth opportunities. It shifts your sense of personal energy and the energy around you into a constant state of abundance. First, you have much more to draw on because you're not wasting it on draining activities or relationships. And, second, you naturally attract those with complementary passions, talents, and goals, which creates situations that multiply capability, teamwork, and results. This, in turn, creates more resources and opportunities, and the energy to go even further.

When you're in your area of Unique Ability and something "bad" happens, you instinctively move toward learning, without a lot of effort or ego being involved. It's like a baby who keeps trying something over and over until they get it, without self-judgment about not succeeding the first time or how long it's taking. If you're not in your Unique Ability, the tendency is to move toward blame, and the feeling is one of effort. But when you're doing something you understand uniquely well, every challenge is an opportunity to learn something new, to go deeper and add to your expertise. Even though you may be working hard, the passion behind it makes it feel relatively effortless. You're doing what you love, and though that might look like work to someone who doesn't share your Unique Ability, to you it's pure self-expression. It's energizing, not draining.

In Unique Ability, there's pleasure in the discovery of something new, not in keeping things rigid and status quo. So sometimes I have a winning day, and sometimes I have a learning day, and both are equally good. Both lead to bigger possibilities for tomorrow. And when you're in the experience of it, you're a perpetual wide-eyed kid in relationship to your own development. It's fascinating and very enjoyable.

The world today is on the side of those who move in the direction of Unique Ability. People want to pay for it. Show me something that commands a premium price, and I'll show you a unique experience that comes from someone practicing their Unique Ability at a high level. Whether it's the work of a great entertainer, athlete, chef, really creative product designer, or even a dentist who has a unique way of addressing the issues in people's lives that begin with their teeth, these are the things people are willing to save up for or pay whatever it takes to have. The world is automating everything repeatable and predictable. Yet, we're a long way from machines being able to replicate the unique self-organizing qualities of Unique Ability in action—the creative, innovative way humans working in their Unique Ability put things together to develop something new, better, and different. Artificial intelligences may have access to every bit of recorded knowledge in the world and every bit of data that sensors can provide, but they lack passion and the educated perception that comes from years of fascinated interest in a certain kind of activity for a certain kind of reason—your Unique Ability activities.

This is why being aware of your Unique Ability is such an advantage: No one else, including the world's smartest machines, knows how you do it. If you take anyone who's been focusing on their Unique Ability for years, they could write a manual about how they do what they do, and others could learn 80 percent of their unique approach. And in fact, our clients often do this. They package and sell their intellectual capital, and it's very valuable to others who've never thought of these things in this way. It can even transform whole industries. The 20 percent they don't teach you is the part where they break their own rules. This is where the magic is. They understand how it all works so well that they can break it, tweak it, change it, and morph it into something even better, something the world has never seen before. It's like an artist learning conventional painting in order to abstract like a genius. You have the potential to be the genius in your own area of Unique Ability. When you're at that level, you never have to worry about selling your knowledge or being copied out of existence—and no competition can touch you. You're in your own realm.

One thing I've been emphasizing lately to my clients is that, with Unique Ability, you're already there. There's no other place or way to be. The seeds of everything you want—all your biggest future results, enjoyment, contribution, meaning, and collaboration—are in this core of talent and passion that's already inside you, informing the very best of what you do. There's no need to go looking for it elsewhere. You need only get really clear on it, and give it the space and resources to thrive and grow by gradually getting rid of everything in your life that doesn't support it. It takes commitment to do this, and it may take courage after that to make the changes in your life that are necessary to support its growth. Sometimes the courage part is unpleasant, and that might deter some people. But if you can just see that as part of the game, you'll soon begin to notice that you develop new capabilities. These are yours to keep and build on. The results they create, the positive feedback from the world, and the sense of progress this generates builds confidence that you can do this and that it's worth it, even if it feels uncomfortable at first. And so you do it again with a bigger-picture view that makes it easier. This is how people make the transition to working at higher and higher levels with their Unique Ability.

Regardless of your age as you pick up this book, you have a future, and the journey into yourself that you're about to take will make that future better in countless ways. Looking back, I can't imagine having lived my life any other way. My sense of being close to the learning sponge I was as a kid of six to ten years old is a lot more powerful today than it was 20 years ago. With what you're about to learn about yourself with this book as your guide, you'll always be in this "zone" in relationship to everything you engage with—continually honing your Unique Ability and how you manifest it out in the world. You never get old to yourself, and you never get bored.

Enjoy the activity and enjoy the evolution. Enjoy the milestones when you see how it's also having a greater impact on those beyond you, and remember that this is all coming from your Unique Ability and your commitment to it. It's just a great way to live.

Dan Sullivan
July 2015

1.

What Is Unique Ability?

Unique Ability®
2.0

Chapter 1

What Is Unique Ability®?

“Be yourself; everyone else is already taken.”

Oscar Wilde

This book is about how to free yourself up to be the very best version of you: the most interesting, rewarding, fun, energizing, exciting, powerful, contributing, creative, unique version by your own standards—encouraged, fueled, and funded by the world’s positive response.

Your Unique Ability is the gateway to this freedom. Could you get through life without discovering it? Certainly. Most people do. But for those who invest the time to focus on this cornerstone of self-knowledge and build their lives around it, the advantages and rewards are immense. Some have described the difference as akin to going from life in black and white to Technicolor.

While it might be said that extraordinary things are always possible, with Unique Ability as your guide, they become predictable. Though we never know exactly how life will unfold (and what fun would it be if you did, really?), the pursuit of a life based on what you love to do and do best, and what you do that creates the most value for others—your Unique Ability—will be the greatest and most rewarding adventure you can embark on. And it will be completely unique to you.

On the course of this journey, you’ll be meeting some of the people we have the great pleasure of knowing, working with, and learning from. You'll hear from a number of our truly amazing clients, all highly successful entrepreneurs who are bravely out in the world using their Unique Abilities to make things better for all of us. This includes Chad Johnson, a positive, can-do thinker whose inspiring Unique Ability story you'll read in a moment. We also hear from our talented teammates whose Unique Abilities shine around us every day.

We're fortunate to work in a culture our leaders, Dan Sullivan and Babs Smith, co-founders of The Strategic Coach Inc., have created that encourages and supports all of us in discovering, using, and strengthening our Unique Ability in every part of our lives.

In fact, this very book is the result of co-author Julia Waller's own Unique Ability. With the whole-hearted encouragement of Dan and Babs, she has developed The Unique Ability Discovery Process built on the Strategic Coach cornerstone concept of Unique Ability, which is the foundation for everything we do. Almost our entire team (beta testers!) and then scores of our clients have benefited from going through this process, guided by Julia's wisdom and passion.

Suspend any disbelief.
What follows might challenge your thinking and how you see and do things now. Parts of it will also be tremendously affirming. At this point, we'll ask you to trust us that the results you'll see from knowing and using your Unique Ability are worth any initially unsettling feelings that a shift in long-held thinking can create. Unique Ability is knowledge that pays off through a lifetime of clearer and better decision-making, and greater ease, momentum, results, and contribution. Once you make the commitment to focus on it, you'll increasingly feel like you're in the right place and doing the right thing.

If you need to make some adjustments to get there, just keep in mind that you're in control of the process, and the world wants your Unique Ability, so when you put it out there that you want to do more of it, solutions often come in unexpected ways.

A word on the foreword.
Before we go any further, we know that many people don't bother to read forewords in books (including us) because we're eager to get to the "really good stuff" later on. No judgment here, but if you happened to skip the foreword by Dan Sullivan on the previous pages, please be good to yourself and go back and read it now. Trust us: Few people create context like Dan, and it's a few minutes with him you won't regret spending before the journey we're about to embark on together. So if you need to, go, and come back. We'll wait here.

A bespoke life.
The promise that Unique Ability holds is really that of a custom-tailored, or "bespoke" life—one that fits you like it was made just for you by an expert, because it is! And you're about to become the expert. Who better than you, after all?

In fact, you probably began this process a long time ago without even knowing it. As we go through the following chapters together, you'll see that there were hints of your Unique Ability showing up early on. You'll come to appreciate these much more as you begin to assemble the pieces of the personal puzzle that is you. Taking the time to understand the concept of Unique Ability more deeply and get a clearer picture of your own, as well as the capacity to see others' (because everyone has one), can accelerate things dramatically, freeing you up to do things you might never have thought possible.

To give you a sense of what this looks like, we'll start with a real story of how a truly remarkable and unique life got built over time.

Anyone who meets Chad Johnson and finds out even a little bit about his life is likely to have a bunch of questions. In fact,

Everywhere in his life, he creates environments that inspire others to ... get out of their shells, take some risks, learn, and experience more joy.

you might not even know where to start. Why is Chad's life so curiosity-inducing? Well, first of all, he has 11(!) children, and a fantastically inspiring relationship with them and with his wife, Jenise. And he has time to run a thriving business with over a hundred employees, in which he's built an enviable company culture. The twist is that it's also located in a different state than the one where Chad and his family live on their working organic farm. He also runs programs for young men and couples, and recently, as of this writing, he began coaching workshops for Strategic Coach.

Though a life this full cannot be without some stresses and challenges, Chad is one of the most genuine, approachable, and obviously happy and grateful people you'll ever meet. Everywhere in his life, he creates environments that inspire others to communicate in a really transparent way—to get out of their shells, take some risks, learn, and experience more joy. He specializes in creating fun unique experiences that have a real "wow" factor. This is the outgrowth of Chad's Unique Ability finding ever more rewarding and valuable ways to show itself in the world. Over the years, he's learned many things about it, at first through observation of what worked and by following what seemed fun and interesting. More recently, it's been by learning about the concept of Unique Ability in The Strategic Coach® Program, and honing his understanding of what his is and where he can take it next.

We use Chad's example because, though his Unique Ability has led him to live a pretty uncommon life, it helps make clear how specific talents and passions that surface early can evolve into bigger and bigger possibilities, and this is common to any Unique Ability. It's just easier to see with a Unique Ability that shows up as unusual.

Childhood clues to Chad's Unique Ability.
For Chad, one of the earliest examples of his unique talents in action was the circus he created as a kid with his siblings and many cousins. With seven siblings plus ten cousins living on either side next door, Chad, though not the oldest, dreamed up the idea and then got everyone excited to be part of a common cause. Among other things, he built a pyramid platform out of wood and got everyone to work together not only to perform, but to sell tickets to the parents and neighbors. But it wasn't just with kids that Chad would do his thing. At family gatherings, reunions, and church events, people got to experience the same thing:

"I was most often the one at the epicenter of creating a fun and dynamic experience for people and making sure they had a great time and a great experience, and I have so many fond memories of growing up because of that. I felt I was really loved and appreciated by most of the people I was around, and that really fed my confidence as a young man that I could help somebody enjoy life more."

On entering the work world as a teen, Chad learned some important lessons about what he was good at and not so good at. His first businesses, a mobile espresso and coffee business, and a cleaning company he started in school, floundered. It wasn't because he couldn't bring people in, but because he was a terrible manager and couldn't put good systems and processes in place. As a pattern, he would have a few seasons of success based on his own effort, charisma, and ability to attract people, but it wasn't sustainable. Employees who loved him as a person would leave because he provided no structure.

A pattern begins to emerge.
After school ended, Chad admits he was "basically clueless" about what to do with his life. He tried all kinds of things and eventually followed a bunch of friends into training for the fire service. It was there that a formative opportunity arose to take these early inclinations and the leadership skills he'd developed as a kid to the next level. At the fire academy, there was an opening for the position of class leader: a student who would help with running the program—getting people to show up on time and fall in, motivating them, and helping get their assignments done. It sounded like a lot of fun to him, so he applied and got the job. It was a revelatory experience.

Says Chad, "I had such a great time during that six- or eight-week program, just bringing that group into a team where they knew every single one of them mattered, was going to be cared for, and was going to experience success. We were going to be the best class they'd ever had at this particular fire academy. It was weird because I didn't really like the fire science stuff. I mean, it was intriguing from the standpoint of learning something new because I like to learn a lot. But the highlight of that time was meeting those men and women, and getting them to become better versions of themselves, if I can be so bold as to say that. I feel like the experience elevated all of us."

He truly enjoyed using his creativity to come up with exercises to help them be successful—things like chants they would do while running that were motivating and inspiring. At the end of the academy, he was at the top of his class academically, and all the captains and instructors who came through affirmed that it was by far the best class they'd seen in 15 years. They credited him with the leadership. He had created a culture where people participated and felt better equipped, and more confident and capable.

A light came on for him in that whole experience. It was pivotal to his thinking about how to apply his talents in the future, not only because the experience was so much fun, but because it also brought success.

Setting things up to win.
After this came the process of getting hired for a real, permanent job in the fire service. While the common strategy for new academy graduates was to apply to lots of different places, Chad decided to make it a game that would favor his strengths by applying to just one, and going deep instead of wide by learning more about that one department than even the chief knew. It worked.

"It was really a fun game for me to go and research every aspect of that department. I went to every station. I met with every captain. I interviewed every person I could in the department. I knew every piece of apparatus. I say all this because going through this process, I learned another part of me: I like to set things up so I can win. I feel like I have an unfair advantage in life because I know if I want something, I know how to go deep and find the right people to ask, 'What do I need to know to get hired here?' I did a lot of work, I built a portfolio, and I felt so equipped and ready. I was so clear, and I knew why I was exactly right for the position.

"I came out of that realizing, 'I can do this in any area of life.' Once I figure out what I want, I have the ability to apply myself to finding everything there is to know about that and seek the counsel of wiser, more experienced people, to gather data and compile it in such a way that it gives me a unique advantage over people who aren't willing to do that work."

Interestingly, this is also the approach he used to court his wife more than 20 years ago. Despite his persistent and determined approach, he jokes that, "by God's grace she fell for my shenanigans."

Chad's heart was in the right place, and he was committed

to loving and caring for Jenise, and building the kind of relationship he had seen and been inspired by as a teen. Fortunately for both of them, she wanted the same thing.

A new realization demands a new path.
By this time, Chad had learned about some of his unique strengths. He knew that he had an ability to connect with people and bring them in, and that this was widely recognized. It was actually what led to his next opportunity.

Despite how much he enjoyed and excelled at his training in the fire service, on taking a permanent role there, Chad discovered quickly that he was in the wrong line of work. A year and a half of employment in the fire service revealed that his natural instinct to innovate to maximize results fell on deaf ears inside that bureaucratic system. He knew it was time to look for something else.

It was at this time that Chad got a call from a broker friend, who invited him out to Colorado to discuss taking a position as his sales and marketing assistant on the basis of his proven ability to connect with and attract people. With Chad's minimal formal education and limited background in finance, it was hardly surprising that the manager at the firm was skeptical. But Chad convinced him to give him a shot against five other candidates (all MBAs in finance from top universities). Off he went to New York to get his Series 7 license, beating all five of the other candidates with his scores, which greatly boosted his confidence.

On his return to Colorado, his friend told him, "Chad, I want you to bring in 20 people that have a million dollars to invest every single month"—a huge goal for any advisor, though Chad didn't know enough to know that at the time. It took him five months to figure it out.

His solution? Track down the most successful broker in Colorado and pester him until he finally gave in and took him to lunch. Then Chad picked his brain. He was the first person in the broker's whole career who had been persistent enough to get him to open up about his wisdom. He was charmed and happy to oblige. Then Chad put a plan in place—admittedly of the "above and beyond" variety—to attract those 20 millionaires a month, and they saw their results shoot through the roof.

Can you see the pattern of past lessons here? Chad knew he was willing and able to do what it takes to succeed, going to lengths others wouldn't. He could count on his creativity to provide memorable unique experiences others would want to be part of, and that would equip them to live richer lives. He knew he had a passion for helping people get what they want and for making everyone and everything around him better. But above all, he knew his relationships were his lifeblood—people mattered greatly to him. He also knew that being "the real Chad"—open, honest, authentic—would strengthen those relationships beyond any measure.

A new challenge a little closer to home.

A couple of years into his financial services partnership, Chad got a call from his dad asking if he'd be interested in joining the family business that his grandfather had started in 1934. After 50 years of hard work, with unfamiliar technology looming on the horizon and market conditions changing, his father and uncle were ready to pass the torch. Chad agreed, on the condition that he got to buy into the business. Within three months, Chad was at the helm. He inherited 60 employees, with morale at an all-time low. The business was providing a decent income, but hardly thriving. He immediately started working on the culture and the team.

He had been feeling stuck until he started putting the right people in the right jobs based on Unique Ability ...

It was at this point that Chad joined The Strategic Coach Program, and started to get much clearer about his Unique Ability and how to build a team around it. He had been feeling stuck until he started putting the right people in the right jobs based on Unique Ability, and learning how to better use his own.

At certain team meetings, Chad's team members fall in, do exercises, and talk about safety, core values, production goals, and what's going on that day. It's positive, upbeat, and motivating. A culture has developed that creates a unique experience for anyone who visits the plant, as well as for everyone who works there. As a result, his brother, on a recent visit to see the company, said he'd hardly recognized the place because it was so different from the pre-Chad days.

Chad uses the same skills he used to court his wife to woo new clients, "It's crazy, but I'll go to such lengths to win others over, create a unique culture and a unique experience, that they don't stand a chance," he says slightly sheepishly. Given enough time, simply by finding out everything about their needs, Chad will do what's necessary to orchestrate a unique experience for them. So far, none have been able to resist giving him their business because they simply want to be a part of the unique culture he's created.

A little S.C.A.M.P. fun gets the job done.

At home, Chad tries to make the most mundane and ordinary tasks into unique, fun experiences. Realizing that chores are not fun, clean-up after dinner with his 11 children takes on the form of something he devised called S.C.A.M.P. (Speedy Clean-Up After Meal Party). By his own admission, it's super corny. (They even have a team cheer and song.) It takes 15 minutes, and in that time, everything gets restored to order.

Chad has realized that his life is permeated with these environments he's created by taking average, routine experiences and trying to make them unique, colorful, and fun. It's also equipping people to see things from a more positive perspective, maximize the situation, and have a bigger picture of the future.

"I see the opportunity to do this in parenting. I see it in marriage. I see it in home life, work life—almost every facet of what I do—and I'm so grateful."

Chad's Unique Ability is "being the real Chad, living life like it's a crazy, fun adventure movie, and inspiring and equipping people to take risks so they can experience richness in the areas that matter most and live their lives with more passion and delight."

Unique Ability's magical rewards.
From having no real notion of what he wanted to do with his life, Chad has been able to figure out how to free himself up to spend the bulk of his work life doing extraordinarily rewarding things, impacting the people he most wants to impact while doing what he loves to do and does best.

This is the magic of Unique Ability and how it frees you up over time, rewarding you for understanding it and making decisions that support it. Your life will be uniquely yours, based on your Unique Ability, and can be just as rewarding for you as Chad's is for him—not to mention all the people around him who benefit when he applies his talents and passion in ways that make their lives better.

Ready to start your Unique Ability journey?
Just like Chad, you have a defining thread of things you've always done, no matter what area of life you look at, that have helped to create successful outcomes. That thread reveals clues that will play a part in leading you to discover your own Unique Ability. Be sure to watch for them as you read on. It's time to delve in and accelerate your progress toward your own most extraordinary and rewarding life.

Unique Ability is the essence of what you love to do and do best.

What is Unique Ability?
So what exactly is Unique Ability, and how can it be so powerful? We'll go back and flesh out the definition and description Dan gave in the foreword to start; then we'll take you through a process to discover and articulate your own. Unique Ability is the essence of what you love to do and do best.

There are four characteristics of Unique Ability:

1. **Superior skill.** It's a superior ability that other people notice and value.
2. **Passion.** You're passionate about using it and want to use it as much as possible.
3. **Energy.** It's energizing for both you and others around you.
4. **Never-ending improvement.** There's a sense of never-ending improvement—you keep getting better and better, and never run out of possibilities for growth.

Because your Unique Ability is fueled by tremendous passion, it can be a very powerful force in the world and create enormous value for others. When you combine passion and talent, you have a recipe for never-ending improvement, energy, excitement, and higher and higher levels of achievement.

Are you sure I have a Unique Ability?
At this point, you may be thinking, "I don't have a Unique Ability. I've never done anything like starting my own circus." At the outset, many people don't see themselves as unique or special; however, by nature, we're all unique. It's a fact of life that there is nobody else in the world just like you. At a very basic level, we're all different. What you choose to do with your uniqueness and your talents is up to you. Not everyone has had a supportive environment like Chad. You may have tried to "fit in" and as a result have downplayed or suppressed your individuality.

Everyone's uniqueness is something to be celebrated and cultivated. What gives your Unique Ability its one-of-a-kind character is that it draws on and combines your innate talents, your personal passion, and your life experience, which no one else can duplicate.

We describe it as an ability because Unique Ability enables you to achieve great results when applied to a range of different activities. It must be used to be seen. Unique Ability shows up exclusively in your interactions with the world. Though the idea of Unique Ability may be a theoretical construct, your actual Unique Ability is very real. It's likely that you apply it in many activities in your life that you love and that give you energy, and yet it is none of these activities on their own. Rather, it's the underlying core that ties them all together. You'll begin to understand this more and see how it applies particularly to you in the chapters that follow and as you work through the exercises in the accompanying Notebook.

Now, if you combine "unique" with "ability," you may be thinking, "Okay, I may be unique, but my abilities really aren't that special." That's the trick with Unique Ability. It comes so naturally and is so easy, fun, energizing, and motivating, we don't think it's special. We think to ourselves, "Can't everyone do that?" The truthful answer is, no, they can't. And certainly not like you do. We're taught to believe that things have to be hard work in order to be valuable. What if we really each have a powerful natural talent and way of operating in the world, that if properly cultivated, expressed, and applied to the right situations could achieve the greatest possible results with relative ease? Doesn't that sound like more fun than continually working on things you're not good at? Unique Ability gives you the chance to do what you love, experience your greatest success, and contribute the most to the world around you.

Another factor that makes it difficult to see your own Unique Ability is that it's mixed in with lots of other things you do. Like most of us, you probably spend a lot of time doing things that simply need to get done to make your life work. You're not passionate about these activities, and you may or may not be great at them—they're just a part of living. Without knowing about Unique Ability, you wouldn't think to differentiate what you love from everything else you do.

After accepting that you have a Unique Ability, the next challenge is figuring out what it is and how to describe it. Getting down to the essence of who you are and what you're about can feel like digging for a needle in a very large haystack, but in fact, it's a creative act. You're drawing from the raw material of your own experience and creating a picture of yourself that answers the question "What is my Unique Ability?" in a way that feels true to you. Often, the way the answers come is like peeling an onion: Each layer takes you a bit deeper and closer to the core, in this case the central essence.

Throughout this book you'll encounter people who, like Chad, and Dan Sullivan in the foreword, got more and more clues over time about the most essential elements of their Unique Ability. They learned by following the sense of enjoyment and energy, recognizing the desire for never-ending improvement, and seeing the positive results whenever these key elements were present.

As with most things in life, if you're willing to delve in and do some thinking, ask questions, and be receptive to what you hear in response, the answer is there. You'll reach a point where you'll say to yourself, "Yes! That's it!" and know you've made progress. The process works every time, as long as you do the work. You just have to be willing to trust it.

What does my Unique Ability look like?
Unique Ability shapes your whole way of being—it's the "you" that makes you who you are. Your Unique Ability shows up in your skills, your talents, your personality characteristics, your activities, your creativity, and your habits. Yet it's more than any of these: It's also an expression of your values. If you've ever felt the excitement of doing something you excel at and others praise you for, something you'd happily keep doing all day long, you've probably experienced your Unique Ability in action. Because you use it so naturally and willingly, it's constantly evolving and improving as you move through life. When you give it room and focus on it, that evolution speeds up and the value you create for others increases, as do the rewards. Some of the rewards of using your Unique Ability with the right audience include money, more opportunities, appreciation, referrals, loyalty, and trust. As you saw in Chad's example, the rewards that motivate you are as personal as your deepest and longest-held desires. You're creating an incredible life being rewarded for what you're naturally compelled to do.

How do I know when I'm using my Unique Ability?
People often don't recognize when they're using their Unique Ability themselves, though others can see it quite clearly. To you, it's so natural that you don't even know you're doing anything special. But when you've seen someone else display their Unique Ability, particularly if they've developed and focused on it over a number of years, it's immediately obvious.

Here are a few things to look for in your daily activities to help you begin to see what comes so naturally: When you use your Unique Ability, time flies. When you're focused on the activities that allow your Unique Ability to come out, you love them so much that you could do them all the time and not run out of energy. In fact, doing these things gives you more energy because you're passionate about them. These activities tap into your internal motivation and drive. You may feel like you're able to access or channel energy and creativity that come from a bigger source, that ideas and solutions just flow naturally.

Think back to your childhood: Was there anything you did endlessly that parents or others had to tear you away from for mundane things like mealtime or sleep? Unique Ability has exactly that quality about it. Some aspect of what you were drawn to back then is likely still part of your Unique Ability today.

Mary Miller, a tremendously inspiring and successful entrepreneur, says with a smile, "Two things I always got in trouble for through my life when I was younger were asking questions and talking too much. And today, that's what I get paid the most for." The essence of your talent has been at play in your life since childhood—Unique Ability is "factory-installed." Chad is still a leader, just on much bigger stages, and Mary gets paid for talking as a sought-after public speaker. After you go through the processes in this book, you can look back and see where your Unique Ability has been in action throughout your life.

The essence of your talent has been at play in your life since childhood—Unique Ability is "factory-installed."

Unique Ability works.
Though it may often feel like play, your Unique Ability doesn't just keep you happily occupied and give you energy—it also works. You generate consistent, high-quality results by using it, and the more you use it, the better you get. It may show up in your work, in your hobbies, in all kinds of relationships, and in the things you do with your family, your community, or your friends. In all these areas, it creates value that others recognize.

The more you understand what your Unique Ability is and how well it works in different situations, the more you can expand your capacity to use it and reap the benefits. You'll have more fun and energy, experience tremendous growth, create meaningful results, and impact others in positive and creative ways. Pretty good for something that comes so easily!

A different world view.
Unique Ability is a philosophy and a way of looking at human potential, beginning with your own and extending to every person in the world. It has many implications for how we view ourselves and others, and provides a unique sense of purpose and direction to our lives. It gives a whole new meaning to the concepts of teamwork and collaboration.

As an idea, it has an infectious quality. Once people understand the concept and begin to see how it operates in their own lives, they feel compelled to share it with others. It offers a different perspective and clarity on issues that many people struggle with. It can even make us feel less alone.

Everyday uniqueness.

One of the most basic tenets of the philosophy of Unique Ability is that having a Unique Ability is just an ordinary part of being human. Everybody has one. In this, we're all equal. What makes it, and you, both special and distinctive is the extent to which you express your Unique Ability, use it to create value, and combine it with the Unique Abilities of others. We each have the choice to do this to a greater or lesser extent and to seek out situations that make it easier or more difficult.

By being aware of other people's Unique Abilities, you gain access to an incredible resource of human capability driven by passion. For many people, a big change in outlook occurs when they begin to accept as a given that everyone has a Unique Ability, and then to appreciate what each person's is. It also means that we can have more acceptance of ourselves and more compassion for others. It frees us from the expectation that we should all be the same with the same level of capability.

When you see this as just part of how the world works, it enables you to tap into and work with your own unique talents and those of others, both on conscious and subconscious levels. Passion is one of the world's greatest untapped energy sources. Unique Ability gives it a productive outlet, and learning to work with Unique Ability allows you to channel and focus it on specific goals and pursue the purposes in life that are most meaningful to you.

The path to freedom and happiness.

The very idea of Unique Ability is liberating because it allows you to be who you are and gives you permission to make your greatest possible contribution to the world by doing what you love to do. It allows you to design the life you want. It also frees each of us from the many negative feelings like fear, guilt, inadequacy, and frustration that arise as we try to do or avoid the things that do not use our Unique Ability.

The flip side to the fact that everyone has a Unique Ability is that everyone also has areas that are not their Unique Ability. Freedom comes from recognizing and letting go of those activities that don't engage your passion and that don't generate energy, superior results, and never-ending improvement.

It's often observed of the world today that people don't suffer from the lack of opportunity; they suffer from too much. They don't have too few options; they have too many. With so many demands on our time and so many choices to be made on a daily basis, understanding your Unique Ability provides a much needed filter, so you can be more decisive and confident about what to do and what not to do. You begin to see more easily when you're on the right path and what you can do to avoid straying off it. Great relief comes from the deep inner sense that by focusing in this way, you're maximizing your happiness, freedom, productivity, and purpose. Keep reading, and we'll show you how to do exactly that.

"Our deepest fear is not that we are inadequate. Our deepest fear is that we are powerful beyond measure. It is our light, not our darkness that most frightens us. We ask ourselves, 'Who am I to be brilliant, gorgeous, talented, fabulous?' Actually, who are you not to be? You are a child of God. Your playing small does not serve the world. There is nothing enlightened about shrinking so that other people won't feel insecure around you. We are all meant to shine, as children do.

> We are born to make manifest the glory of God that is within us. It's not just in some of us; it's in everyone. And as we let our own light shine, we unconsciously give other people permission to do the same. As we are liberated from our own fear, our presence automatically liberates others."
>
> **Marianne Williamson, *A Return to Love*[1]**

THE BOTTOM LINE:

- Unique Ability is your talent, driven by your passion—it's what you love to do and do best.
- Everyone has one, so you don't need to be good at everything. There are others who will love to do the things you have no talent for.
- Unique Ability is "factory-installed" and so natural you most likely don't even realize you're using it.
- It's the best way to create consistent, high-quality results in everything you do, and it keeps getting better the more you use it.
- You'll be able to use it as a filter to focus on your best opportunities and stay on the path that best suits your talents.

1 Excerpt from pp. 190-1 ["Our deepest fear ... liberates others."] from A RETURN TO LOVE by MARIANNE WILLIAMSON. Copyright (c) 1992 by Marianne Williamson. Reprinted by permission of HarperCollins Publisher.

2.

Discovering Your Unique Ability

Unique Ability®
2.0

Chapter 2

Discovering Your Unique Ability

"Knowing yourself is the beginning of all wisdom."

Aristotle

We are all unique, even if we don't know it.
It's time to discover and define your Unique Ability. Perhaps you're one of a small number of people who already have a sense of what your Unique Ability is and are using it consciously on a regular basis. Most people, however, don't even realize they have a Unique Ability. One of the trickiest things about Unique Ability is that it's remarkably difficult to see our own because being so close to our own uniqueness makes it very difficult to appreciate. We've come to refer to this paradox as "Unique Ability blindness."

Because our Unique Ability comes so easily to us, we tend to believe that everyone can do the same thing as we can and that it's no big deal. You're just being you, doing what comes naturally, doing what anyone would do, right? Nothing could be further from the truth.

Most people can't do what you do at all, and even those with a somewhat similar ability have their own unique way of doing it, are fueled by their own purpose, and bring their own set of unique experiences to bear.

So the next time someone praises you for doing something that feels easy or not all that special, ask yourself, "Am I using my Unique Ability?" In doing so, you'll begin to overcome one of the first obstacles that stands in the way of discovering and articulating your Unique Ability: the tendency we each have to downplay or overlook it altogether.

> "One of the stumbling blocks for some is the word 'unique.' Unique implies something very special, very out of the ordinary. And at the core, Unique Ability is all of these things, but it is also so instinctive and so natural that often we are the last people to know."
>
> **Adrienne Duffy**

A fish with tennis shoes.
Christine Kane, one of our clients, came up with this way to describe this blindness:

"It's like you're a goldfish in a huge pond, and you can't really see the water around you because water is all you know. The Unique Ability Process is like giving a pair of tennis shoes to that fish. You finally get to jump out of the pond and look back in at yourself and see all that water!"

For some people, seeing their whole selves from this new perspective of uniqueness can be confronting. Suddenly, the conventional path of working on your weaknesses rather than on your strengths seems ill-fitting. If we downplay our own power and talents, it's easier to stay comfortable. We don't need to make changes or take risks that might seem scary at first; we can hide out in the pack believing we are like everyone else. So the blindness sometimes gets reinforced by fear of change, of which we may not even be conscious. Thankfully, after many years of helping thousands of entrepreneurs, their team members, their families, and countless others to focus on their Unique Ability, we've discovered some effective ways to get around these obstacles.

In this section, we're going to introduce you to *two* well-tested and proven paths to identify your Unique Ability. Together, they make up The Unique Ability Discovery Process. We highly recommend you do both parts, as they each provide useful and different results. However, you have a choice of where to begin, which we'll explain next. The best results will come from picking the path that most resonates with you, The Activities Path or The Naming Path.

Quick and practical: Take The Activities Path.
The Activities Path is the faster process. If you start here, you'll take a close look at the activities you spend your time on, and you'll figure out which use your Unique Ability and which don't. We'll walk you through a set of simple exercises that will give you a basic understanding of the concept of Unique Ability and show you how to use it to create immediate strategies for positive change in your life. You'll get insight into your Unique Ability as it shows up in what you do now. And, you'll also start to recognize the benefits of doing more of the things that give you an opportunity to use your Unique Ability and fewer of the things that don't. It's a great place to start. For relatively little effort, and in a short time, you can begin to change your thinking and actions and see immediate results.

For fast, practical, actionable results right now, start with The Activities Path. You can do the first couple of exercises in an hour or two and come away with some immediate insights and improvement ideas. Or you can take more time if you choose.

Dig deeper: Take The Naming Path.
If you want a more specific, powerful, and articulated understanding of your Unique Ability, you'll want to dig deeper to actually figure out what this Unique Ability of yours is. The Naming Path will take you there. Here, you'll gather feedback and insights from several outside perspectives and do some self-inquiry to arrive at a clear statement of your Unique Ability. You'll describe *what* you're doing that creates such great value for everyone around you, and *why* you do it.

We'll walk you through all the steps of what's essentially a course in how to identify and articulate your own unique set of talents and the passion that drives them. With our 25-plus years of coaching expertise to guide you, you'll be able to focus just on gathering the raw material and doing the thinking. It can be done in a few weeks, or months, depending on how fast you want to go.

Because this deep-dive approach was originally designed to work for busy entrepreneurs (though many other kinds of people have done it since) and keep their interest, every step along the way is engaging, worthwhile, and has its own rewards. You'll see and feel the progress along the way!

Discovering your Unique Ability is not a spectator sport!

Whatever you do, DO!
While tremendous benefits can be had from following either of these two paths on their own, the people who have had the biggest breakthroughs and transformations have done both. If you prefer to ease your way in, start with The Activities Path and use what you learn from it as raw material for the naming and defining you'll do throughout The Naming Path.

Or, if you're up to the challenge and are keen to know exactly what your Unique Ability is, jump into The Naming Path first. The results you come up with will make The Activities Path more meaningful, and you'll be even more motivated to free yourself up.

But wherever you decide to start (and ultimately it doesn't really matter), we urge you to choose at least one of the paths and DO it. Discovering your Unique Ability is not a spectator sport! Anyone who's gone through the Discovery Process will tell you that all the benefit is in doing the work to really figure out your Unique Ability, and putting it in use. This is a

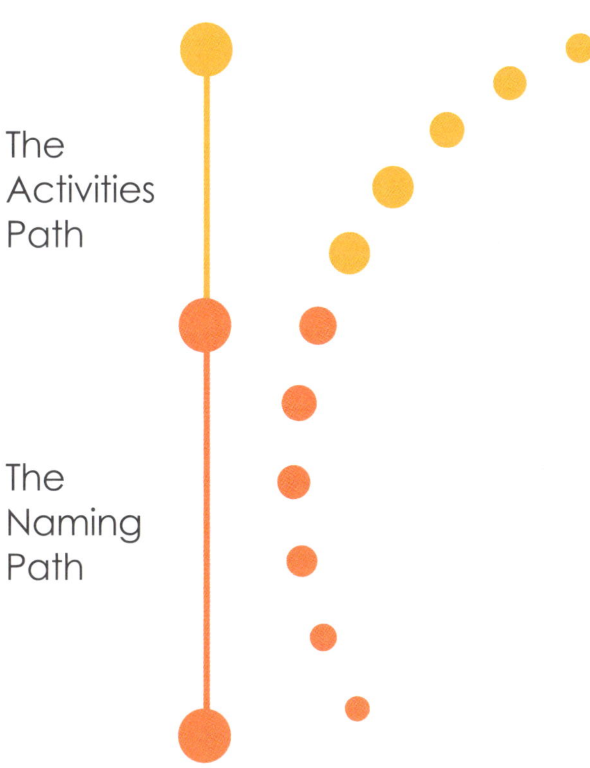

highly interactive book. It's a lot more fun and it makes a lot more sense when you're working with your own examples and having your own personal insights and breakthroughs. Just reading about it is like smelling great food without being able to eat it: It'll just leave you hungry and unsatisfied!

So, let's get started.

The Unique Ability Notebook.
As you read this book, we're going to walk you through a series of thinking exercises. We'll ask you questions and guide you through a conversation about your special talents. To help make your journey easier, we've designed a Notebook specifically for this unique thinking process. Your Unique Ability Notebook will become a rich storehouse of knowledge, insights, and wisdom that you can refer back to, refine, and add to over time. It has been scientifically proven that handwriting helps the brain absorb and retain more, so doing these exercises with pencil (or pen) and paper is highly recommended. You may also want to type up some of your work to facilitate editing, refinement, and sharing of your Unique Ability.

The symbol on the left below (a circle with a page number inside) is a heads-up that we're giving you the context for filling out an exercise. It will guide you to the correct page in the Notebook each time.

6 **Exercise: What's My Purpose?**
It's a lot easier to do anything when you're really clear on the purpose and intended results. The first exercise in the Notebook, What's My Purpose, will help you articulate why you're doing the work to discover your Unique Ability and what you hope to gain as a result. Go to page 6 in the Notebook now to get started. Being clear on your intentions and writing them down is the perfect way to lay a solid foundation for what you're about to do as you read on.

3.

The Activities Path

The Activities Path

A.1 The Activity Inventory

A.2 The Activity Snapshot

A.3 The Unique Ability Action Plan

A.4 The One-Year Goal

Chapter 3

The Activities Path

Part of what keeps us from seeing our Unique Ability is that it's camouflaged among all the other things we do.

This path is made up of a series of exercises you can do fairly quickly to distinguish *what is* your Unique Ability from *what's not*, using all the things you do right now as the raw material.

Very quickly, you'll get a sense of where your Unique Ability is showing up in your day-to-day activities—which parts of what you do engage your Unique Ability and which don't. This consciousness will help you make better decisions about what to do more of and what to do less of. It also makes it easier to understand your Unique Ability better over time. You'll become more aware of when you're using it and pay more attention to what that feels like and the results it creates, versus what it feels like to not be working in your Unique Ability.

Strategic Coach client Paul VanDuyne says, "You're able to craft a much better direction and use of your time. You make some clear decisions on what makes sense to continue and what makes sense to either stop or delegate."

To illustrate the tremendous power of The Activities Path over time, we can look at the growth of Strategic Coach, from an idea in the minds of Dan Sullivan and Babs Smith in 1989, to the $30M company it is today. Though Dan understood the basic concept of Unique Ability even before he met Babs, it was her recognition and talent for being able to strip away non-Unique Ability activities from him that really freed up his Unique Ability to flourish, and the company to grow as a result.

Babs recalls from the early days, "We could tell which activity was peeled off and when. There would be jumps in confidence and productivity. So somewhere along the line, Dan coined the term Unique Ability and started talking about why it's so valuable to peel away the stuff that isn't your Unique Ability." Right away, Babs recognized that, "even if you don't know what your Unique Ability is, you know what it isn't. If you're still bogged down in *that*, you won't have the attention and

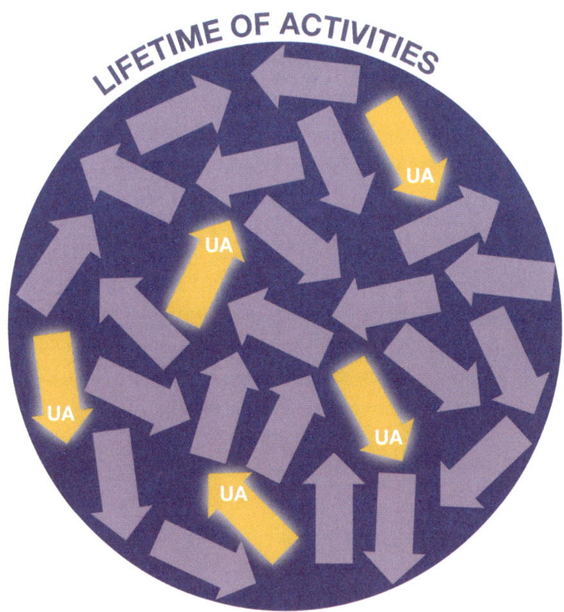

energy to zero in on the fun stuff." For Dan, at the beginning, that meant giving up chasing down checks, hand-drawing and coloring his own worksheets for clients, and making sales calls.

Gradually over time, as the business grew and he took on new responsibilities, those too would get "peeled off" as they became more routine, unnecessary, or simply better done by others. Driving was replaced by a car service. Creating new content for certain workshop groups was taken over by team members. Dan has been freed up from these, and others, in order to look for and multiply Unique Ability in other people, including many game-changing entrepreneurs, who are in turn making a much bigger impact on the world as a result.

The approach you're about to learn is one that Babs has used with many Strategic Coach team members to do for them what she has always done for Dan. The bonus with learning these exercises is that they can be used over and over again. They'll become new tools in your toolbox for anytime you want to transform feelings of overwhelm, boredom, being "stuck," uncertainty, and lack of motivation into excitement, freedom, positive energy, momentum, and confidence about the future.

It's very normal, even for people who are growing, to get stuck on a plateau every once in a while where it feels difficult to get to the next level. It's reassuring to know that this may be just a sign that you're ready to shed some more activities that are not your Unique Ability. Once you've done these exercises, you'll be able to do them anytime you feel the need for a new breakthrough to get yourself confident, positive, and moving again.

THE BOTTOM LINE:

- Follow The Activities Path to distinguish which activities use your Unique Ability and which don't.
- Free yourself from the activities that aren't using your natural talents so you can better see and understand what does make up your Unique Ability.
- Revisit The Activities Path anytime you're feeling stuck or want to take things to the next level.

The Activity Inventory™

A cross-section of your life.
Your Unique Ability is expressed through a variety of activities in your life. The positive feedback, enjoyment, and energy you get from activities that use your Unique Ability make you want to do these things more and get even better at them. Yet we all do many things every day that don't engage our Unique Ability.

The Activity Inventory is a simple exercise designed to capture as many of your daily activities as possible and look at them through a new Unique Ability lens. It's like taking a cross-section or a core sample of your life and analyzing it. No matter what you do for a living (or not) or where you are in your life, this exercise gives you a close-up view of how you're really spending your time and a better understanding of your talents—and what you enjoy and don't enjoy doing. What seems like a simple process provides a surprising amount of insight.

Notebook Exercise A.1: The Activity Inventory.

Your raw material: List all the things you do every day.
Start by making a list of the things you do in the course of your daily routine. Separate work (whatever you consider your work; for example, volunteering) or school from your personal life to get a clear picture of each. Look at the "micro" scale of your activities—daily tasks like having phone conversations with clients, solving people problems, answering email,

sample

STRATEGIC COACH®

The Activity Inventory™

Work

1. Emails – problem-solving
2. Emails – scheduling
3. Client correspondence
4. Giving presentations
5. Face-to-face client meetings
6. Scheduling appointments
7. Hosting company meetings
8. Researching specifics
9. Researching new ideas
10. Business reading
11. Strategy vision sessions
12. Solving problems – clients
21. Organizing my projects
22. Negotiating contracts
23. F/up on project status
24. Reviewing financials
25. Mentoring team members
26. Travel arrangements
27. Meeting w/ direct reports
28. Connecting w/ the team
29. Marketing strategy
30. Marketing projects
31. Setting company goals
32. Developing sales plan

researching, designing, planning events, building, fixing things, caregiving, writing, studying, or whatever you do in your professional, "work," or student life. As you write them down, break them into discrete activities as much as possible. For instance, "emails" might be broken down into different kinds of emails that involve different kinds of activities or different people. Perhaps you love responding to emails that involve helping people solve a problem, but get stressed out by emails that involve scheduling or giving people information. List each of these as separate activities.

If you want to tackle your whole life, make a list of personal activities as well (cooking, managing finances, yard work, and all of the particulars of your day). Aim for a fairly broad list of examples, but don't get too carried away.

Come up with as many things as you can as they occur to you. You may want to carry your Inventory around with you for a week or longer, since you likely do lots of things you might not think of including at first. Imagine a day, from the time you wake up in the morning to the time you go to bed—for both weekdays and weekends—and chronicle as many of your activities as possible. Next, expand your scope to a month or a year. Perhaps there are bigger projects you've worked on in the past or that lie ahead that belong on your list. Don't worry about writing them in any particular order; it doesn't matter. Our examples will give you an idea of what to include.

If there are any activities that you're new at or have very little experience with, leave them off your list for now. It's probably too soon to accurately judge your feelings or results in these areas, which will make them difficult to categorize in the next step. Activities may also come to mind that you'd like to do, but aren't doing now. Capture these if you'd like, but keep them separate as "wish list" items. Hopefully, you'll be able to free up some time to do some of these as a result of doing this exercise. Go and list your activities in your Notebook now.

Categorize your list into four types of activities.
Now that you've got a picture of how you're spending your time, we're going to introduce you to a different way of looking at your activities, categorizing each by how it relates to your Unique Ability. We'll use four categories—Unique, Excellent, Competent, and Incompetent—to create some important distinctions. After reading the following descriptions, you're going to place the letter U, E, C, or I—representing the appropriate category—beside each activity on your Activity Inventory list.

Here are the descriptions of each category:

U = Unique Ability Activities
• Superior skill • Passion • Energy • Never-ending improvement
Of the activities on your list, which are your favorites, the ones you do exceedingly well and really love to do? Which also really

tap into your passion and make you happy? We're defining your "sweet spot" activities now. You feel a buzz of excitement when you engage in these. You're in what positive psychologists have described as "Flow" or "the Zone," which is loosely defined as "the mental state of operation in which a person performing an activity is fully immersed in a feeling of energized focus, full involvement, and enjoyment in the process of the activity." (Wikipedia)

Others around you would agree that you show superior skill in these areas. These activities create more energy than they use up, and you might energize other people as you do them. When you're engaged in these activities, you lose track of time.

Look at these activities and ask yourself: Could I pretty much do this all day long and still keep going? Do I feel like I'm "on my game"? If it's part of your job, would you still want to do it even if you didn't get paid for it? If you've received any training or instruction in this area, you were probably a star student because you've got a natural ability here. You would love to spend your time getting even better. There are always new and exciting possibilities for improvement, no matter how good you get.

"When you're connecting with certain kinds of activities, you just feel it. You know that there's something there that percolates the energy, and the passion comes into it. For me as a young girl, the first time I really experienced that was playing music. I picked up a flute, I started to play, and I just had a natural instinct to do it. I got it quickly, and it was relatively straightforward for me. Plus I loved the learning and the challenge! You could say that was a Unique Ability activity. Of course, I didn't have the words for it then, but you just gravitate towards it."

Adrienne Duffy

E = Excellent Activities

• Superior skill • No passion • Reputation • Teamwork

The biggest difference between Unique Ability and Excellent activities is your lack of passion. Similar to Unique Ability activities, you demonstrate a superior ability, but deep down, you don't have a real sense of enjoyment when doing these things. Of your activities, which do you recognize as something you do better than most people but you don't love doing? You've got a superior skill, so you probably find accomplishing these activities satisfying. You create results, which can be rewarding. People count on you for what you're able to do in this area. You may have developed a reputation for your ability. Many people want you to work with or for them, and they provide you with opportunities to do these things. There's a great sense of teamwork: People want to work with you because your abilities meet a very high standard.

Despite your success, however, you don't really want to do more of these activities. You may even feel trapped because they take up so much of your time and keep you from doing more of the "fun stuff." They fall short in the passion department and don't give you energy. Perhaps you loved them at one point in time, but now you find them boring, and they no longer hold any challenge or interest for you. For all the external advantages, these activities leave you feeling less than excited. If you spend too much time on them at the expense of Unique Ability, you may be thinking, "Is this all there is?"

C = Competent Activities

• Meet minimum standards • Anxiety • Competition
• Repetition

There are other activities on your list where your skill level is merely adequate—you only reach minimum standards, and a lot of other people could do these activities much better and with a lot less effort. You are simply average. You worry about falling behind, failing, or becoming obsolete. Because you aren't distinct from others, you face a lot of competition. The activities seem the same, day after day, so things feel monotonous. You don't feel inspired to get better, and your efforts don't bring you any kind of growth. There is little or no improvement in your performance over time. You struggle to get these activities done. They drain your battery and require a lot of concentrated energy just to get a mediocre result.

I = Incompetent Activities

• Failure • Conflict • Stress • Avoidance

It's often most clear where your Unique Ability isn't. Which activities would you be happy never to do again because you experience failure? Which make you feel anxious because you're simply not good at them? You've put a lot of time and effort into these, but you still don't get a good result. Nothing

1	Emails – problem-solving	E
2	Emails – scheduling	I
3	Client correspondence	C
4	Giving presentations	U

seems to work, and you can't make headway. If you were going to be good at them, you would be by now—but it's just not happening. You might also find yourself in conflict with others when you're doing these things because of your low skill level. Breakdowns in communication occur frequently. Everything is difficult. You experience stress because these activities take up a lot of mental energy, mostly because you're worried about them not being done or not being done well. You put off, procrastinate, or avoid these activities as much as possible because you find them so difficult to do. They are completely energy-draining and demoralizing.

While it might be hard to acknowledge, everyone has activities they're incompetent at and that's okay. Being honest about them is the starting point for creating a more enjoyable life.

What about "hobbies"?

Occasionally, someone will come across an activity they love to do but would only categorize as Competent or Incompetent in terms of skill—we call this a "hobby." Some of our clients have put activities like golf, gardening, cooking, or dancing in this category.

A hobby golfer, though they may not be very talented, might still enjoy being out on the course, the social aspects of the game, and the relief it gives them from their busy lives. If you find that you have a hobby on your list, you may want to see if there is a business aspect to it and categorize that part. For example, business people doing deals on the golf course would include this part of golfing as an important activity on their list. However, if skill really isn't an issue, either because the activity requires no skill, or because you don't strive to develop your capabilities since it's just a hobby that you do for other reasons, just leave it off your list altogether.

Some tips as you categorize.

- **Tell the truth.** It's important to tell the truth about your ability level or lack thereof. You don't need to be good at everything. If you're not sure you have superior skill, think of what others who interact with you (your boss, clients, family) would say and use that as your standard. If you don't excel at it, be honest. Most people err on the side of being hard on themselves. They will often designate an activity as Competent when, in fact, they're working at an Excellent level.

- **Resist the urge to strategize.** As you categorize, try to keep yourself from jumping ahead to think about what you're actually going to do about it. Just categorize for now. You'll be able to choose what actions you take, if any, in the next steps.

- **Skill differentiates Excellent from Competent.** Just because you don't like an activity doesn't mean you're not good at it. Sometimes Excellent activities are very frustrating because they take you away from doing things that fall into your Unique Ability—but that doesn't detract from your skill level. If you do it well and accurately, and do a great job, it fits in the Excellent bucket. If you don't, it probably belongs in Competent.

- **Consider your audience.** If an activity feels like it belongs under Excellent sometimes and Unique other times, it may be because doing it with a certain audience juices you up, while doing it with others saps your enthusiasm. So consider who you're working with as part of the equation. It might just be about who you're doing it for, and this is a great thing to get clear about! You may find you can work toward doing it more with the audience that gives you energy and less with those that don't.

- **Refining your distinctions.** If something feels like a mixture of two categories for any reason, see if you can break it apart and qualify when (under what circumstances) or what part of it might make it fall into one category versus another. For instance, if planning events is on your list, you might realize that choosing the venue and creating ambience get you really excited. Perhaps you can create party experiences that no one else can match because you love it and go that much further than anyone else would. That's obviously a Unique Ability activity. On the other hand, the logistics of managing and coordinating the caterers and all the suppliers may seem more stressful and draining. If, though, you're still good at it, and you're mostly just relieved when it's over and everything went off with no glitches, that's probably more of an E (Excellent) or even a C (Competent). To add a little flexibility for those who need it, we do sometimes use E+/- or C+/- in the categories, so do that if it helps.

  For the event planner example above, maybe planning weddings is really enjoyable, but planning corporate events is less satisfying. Even though they use very similar skills, you still get more energy from helping people create a once-in-a-lifetime dream event with the potential for stories and memories that will be talked about for generations, whereas another meeting is just that. In that case, you would make them separate activities and label one a U and one an E. This is an example of understanding the effect your audience has on your enjoyment, described in the previous point.

- **What not to categorize, yet.** If it's a "wish list" activity, label it as such for future reference, but don't categorize unless it's obvious to you where it fits.

16 **Notebook Exercise A.1: Categorize your activities.**

Go ahead and take some time now to go back through your Activity Inventory and categorize your activities. Mark each item as follows:

U = Unique Ability activities
E = Excellent activities
C = Competent activities
I = Incompetent activities

THE BOTTOM LINE:

- List all the activities that take up your time, both personally and professionally.
- Classifying your activities as Unique Ability, Excellent, Competent, or Incompetent quickly shows you which activities use your best talents and which don't.
- It's important to be honest about your skill level and passion. It's okay to say you have Incompetent activities, just like it's okay to say that something is your Unique Ability.
- Your audience matters—sometimes changing who you're being with can make all the difference.

The Activity Snapshot™

Once you've categorized your activities, the next simple step is to reorganize and rewrite them by category. By doing this, you'll see a clear snapshot of what's in each of your areas—Unique Ability, Excellent, Competent, and Incompetent—and get a sense of how you're really spending your time.

Notebook Exercise A.2: The Activity Snapshot.

Create your snapshot in time.
Take the activities listed in each of your work and personal Activity Inventories and write them in the box that corresponds to each category.

The **Activity Snapshot**™

Work

Unique Ability® Activities (• Superior skill • Passion • Energy • Never-ending improvement)	Excellent Activities (• Superior skill • No passion • Reputation • Teamwork)
- Company meetings	- Emails – problem-solving
- Strategic thinking & vision	- Writing reports
- Giving presentations	- Team problem-solving
- Client problem-solving	- Reviewing financials
- Negotiating	- Marketing projects
- Mentoring, relationship-building	- Developing sales plans
- Creating & reinforcing the culture	- Dealing with lawyers
- Reading & learning & researching ideas	- Creating presentations
- Goal-setting	
25 %	40 %
Competent Activities (• Meet minimum standards • Anxiety • Competition)	**Incompetent Activities** (• Failure • Conflict • Stress)

As you do this, if you see a common theme or pattern, feel free to group or summarize similar activities together under a subheading. For instance, if the Unique Ability activities on your Inventory include “fixing the toaster” and “figuring out what’s wrong with the car,” you might summarize these as “mechanical work” or “fixing things” on your Activity Snapshot. If you want to write each activity separately, that’s also fine if you prefer that level of specificity.

Calculate how much time you’re spending in each category. Look at your overall Snapshot of activities, calculate approximately what percentage of time you’re currently spending in each quadrant and write this down. Omit any “new” and “wish list” activities. Some people total up hours over a certain time frame (say a week or a month), while others just estimate off the top of their heads. This isn’t a precise science, so don’t worry if you only come up with a very rough number.

What you’re doing is creating your own measurement system, so do whatever makes the most sense to you. At this stage, you just want a ballpark percentage to give you a sense of the bigger picture. This will also give you a baseline, so when you look back three, six, or 12 months from now, you can do a new Snapshot and see how much progress you’ve made.

Please *don’t worry* if your numbers aren’t where you’d like them to be at this stage! Even if you’re not working much in your Unique Ability yet or if you’re spending too much time in your Competent or Incompetent areas, just doing this exercise has given you the awareness to begin to do something about it. In fact, you may already be having ideas and insights about what you want to change.

If your numbers do look great, congratulations! You’re doing a great job at aligning your life with your Unique Ability. Wherever you're at now, you'll have a chance to look at improvement ideas and ways to fine-tune your current situation in the next step of the process.

THE BOTTOM LINE:

- Your Snapshot gives a quick overview of how you're spending your time.
- Group similar activities together and summarize your activities by category—Unique, Excellent, Competent, and Incompetent.
- Estimate what percentage of time you're spending in each category, in both your personal and professional life.
- Your Snapshot isn't good or bad. It's merely a reflection of where you're at now.

The Unique Ability® Action Plan

Okay. Now for the fun part—using what you've done to transform your life for the better! The Activity Snapshot lets you see your activities in a new way that starts your thinking about what you can do differently to free up your time and energy. Here, we'll help you create a basic plan so you can start to increase the time you spend in your Unique Ability and decrease the time you spend doing everything else. Sound good?

Operating within a Unique Ability framework means finding ways to let go of what you're not good at. It's time to give yourself permission to give up doing things that are not your Unique Ability. Yes—it is okay to do that! It also means being resourceful and looking for complementary talents and abilities to free you up.

Of course, labeling something an Incompetent or Competent activity is not an excuse to be irresponsible about your commitments, nor are we suggesting that you try to let go of everything overnight (though many people want to once they realize how much time they're spending doing things they're neither passionate about nor good at).

The mantra here, and throughout this process, is "progress, not perfection." Take as much time as you need to transform your situation comfortably and responsibly. Every little step will make a difference. Some changes may be easy and quick to implement, but others may take a good deal of thinking, planning, and preparation. That's completely normal. Use your vision of having a Unique Ability-filled life as inspiration for what's possible, and consider where you are today as ground zero. One day, you'll look back and be amazed by your incredible progress.

Start at the bottom: Competent and Incompetent.
The first thing to do is to take a look at everything on the bottom half of your Activity Snapshot page, the Competent and Incompetent sections. They're the "red alert" areas that if unattended could lead to failure or conflict. Think of these as areas where your job is to fire yourself (nicely, of course!). Figuring out how to stop doing everything in these two areas (most people start with Incompetent as these can weigh heavily on your mind) is usually the most urgent because you're experiencing a huge amount of stress, given the fact that your skill level is so low.

You may feel as though you "should" get better at these things, but, truthfully, the amount of time, energy, money, and other people's investment it would take to improve isn't worth it. It's not part of your factory-installed talent. Your resources will be much better put to use supporting the growth and development of your Unique Ability.

Keep in mind, also, that if you're doing any of these things in your professional life, you're likely costing your organization time and money. Are you really going to create value doing things you're not good at? It's highly unlikely. Undoubtedly, there's a much better use for your talent and expertise, and you may be able to make a very compelling case for getting these activities off your plate.

Starting with Incompetent and Competent activities is also the quickest way to regain energy. In any area of your life, doing things you're not good at will leave you feeling drained and unproductive. On the flip side, any time and energy freed up by not doing these things can be redirected toward focusing on your Excellent and Unique Ability activities. You'll then create much better results and be a lot more satisfied.

Five ways to free yourself.
To expand your creative thinking about what the options are, here are five ways you might be able to strip away some of your tougher or less desirable activities. Be resourceful and see if you can apply any of these suggestions to your situation:

1. **Stop doing it.** If it's not really that important, you may be able to just stop doing it without any negative consequences. If you think it's wise, try dropping it and see if it makes a difference to anyone. Sometimes people don't even notice!

2. **Delegate it.** You can delegate the activity if you can find someone else to do it. Can you pay someone else to do it for you? This often doesn't have to cost a lot. Many people find students or family members to do research, organize things, do repairs or cleanups, or other tasks for them. Crowd-sourcing or online solutions are abundant and are great resources to tap into. It's easier than ever to find people to do even small tasks (now sometimes referred to as "micro jobs") for a reasonable fee. Many websites allow you to pitch a job and receive responses from people who want that kind of work. There are sites for everything from household tasks and errands, to design work and administrative assistance. If you've never looked at one of

these sites and you're curious, browse through the listings on *fiverr.com* to see the kinds of diverse things people will do for you for what's usually a very affordable fee.

3. **Swap it.** Another option is to trade this activity with someone else in exchange for something you'd rather do and they'd rather not.

4. **Automate it.** Sometimes using technology to automate an activity can be worthwhile to get it off your plate. With mobile devices and apps, robotics, and the Internet, the number of possibilities for getting the same results in different ways with the help of technology is growing every day. Simple, repetitive tasks like weekly grocery shopping or bill-paying can easily be automated now, but there are many more possibilities becoming accessible and affordable. For instance, some of our offsite team members have been using Beam robots (like a Skype conversation on a robot base you can drive around) as a way to be present remotely at meetings, saving hours and thousands of dollars on flights. Even aspects of your thinking can be automated today. If you're really bad at remembering things or being on time, there's an app (or several hundred) for that!

5. **Transform it.** If it really needs to happen, and you don't have anyone else to take it off your plate, see if there's a way to change when or how you get it done. For example, if it's something like cooking, can you plan to do batch-cooking on the weekend and freeze meals so they're ready? Or, if you need to write thank-you cards to clients, but you'd rather be on the phone, write one in between every energizing phone call until they're done.

Even excellence doesn't make the cut.
The benefit of getting rid of Competent and Incompetent activities is usually pretty clear. After all, finding ways to eliminate things that cause stress, frustration, or boredom is often fun and a great relief. Ultimately, however, you will even want to eliminate Excellent activities.

"Really?" you say, "But I'm *good* at those!"

Yes, really! While this advice may surprise you, often the biggest thing holding a person back from extraordinary achievements is their clinging to what's *merely really good* (and, frankly, uninspiring). This might seem counter to what you've always believed because a lot of successful people make a good living doing mostly Excellent activities.

The Excellence Trap.
Plain and simple: Excellent activities can take up a lot of time, and we can get stuck doing them. It's such a common occurrence that we've named this "The Excellence Trap." You may get praised and rewarded well for doing these activities because you're really talented and you produce great results, so the temptation is strong to keep doing them. They're *safe*, even if they're not particularly exciting or passion-inducing. Still, your efforts would be better invested in Unique Ability activities, where, paradoxically, you have the greatest room for improvement.

Your Unique Ability is an area where you can keep having breakthrough after breakthrough, keep feeling excited, and keep creating valuable results long past the point where others lose steam. Unique Ability is also an endlessly renewable resource. If you want to keep increasing the size of your contribution and the impact of your talents, you'll eventually need to create room by getting rid of some of your Excellent activities.

This doesn't have to happen overnight or all at once. It can be a gradual, well-planned and -executed transition, if that's what makes the most sense. What matters is that you commit to it and follow through. It may feel like a leap of faith at first, but once you let go of an Excellent activity to make space for a Unique Ability activity, you'll see there's no turning back.

For Stuart Poonawala, understanding Unique Ability gave him the insight to see the dynamic behind a pattern in his life he'd been experiencing and trying to understand for years: "I'd have great energy for a new role or a new job, and then over time I'd get bored with it, and then I'd want to seek new things to keep myself interested. I was always getting into trouble because the bank [his employer at the time] wanted me to knuckle down and do what I was supposed to be doing, and I was always trying to find new things instead. I think I eventually became bored with getting bored, and that's what led me to leave and do my own thing. Again, I had a lot of energy around the new business ... some days I'd be really energetic and enthused, but then other days I'd be really bored. I went through my early career and the early part of my business not understanding why I was feeling this way. People would say I was impatient or had a low boredom threshold, and I always thought, you know, that doesn't feel right."

After going through the process in this book, Stuart began to realize that creativity was an essential part of his Unique Ability. "That so resonated. If I'm creating, I'm never bored. At the point at which I've created something, I lose interest in it. Once I understood the concept of Unique Ability and started to develop it, it gave me permission to be who I am and to set up everything around that. I completely understand my past now, how I've become bored with things, and even why I've gotten in trouble at school. My wife takes great pleasure in showing my children my early school reports. The kids love it when they see teachers writing, 'Stuart has great potential, if only he would actually apply it ...'

"Now it tells me how I need to operate within my business in order to feed my creativity. As long as I'm being creative, the business will move forward. I'll be happy and will never need to do anything different. What it's also shown me is that, as an entrepreneur, I can stay in business until I die because I'm always going to be creating as long as my mind is active. It takes me out of the mindset of a job, which is bureaucratic, into a world of endless possibilities—because how can I ever limit myself in being creative?"

Identifying his Unique Ability helped Stuart find the core of what will keep him fascinated and motivated for the rest of his life. He can now build the rest of his life around it rather than struggling to do things he was skilled at but clearly not passionate about.

Ditch the guilt.

It's pretty natural to assume that if you don't like doing something, others must not like it either. Natural, but untrue. It's also often a difficult idea to shake, even if you intellectually understand that everyone has a Unique Ability and, by definition, that means it's different than yours (or it wouldn't be unique). This assumption, whether it's conscious or not, can lead to feelings of guilt about delegating. We're going to be very frank about this. If this is what you're thinking, get over it! If you've seen the Bob Newhart skit, do as he says and "Stop it!" (If you don't know what we're talking about, Google it: "Bob Newhart stop it video" and once you're done laughing, please come back.)

If you feel guilt about relinquishing the tasks you dislike, think about it this way: By delegating, you're giving someone else who likes this activity the opportunity to do more of it and possibly even get paid for doing it. Or to put it even more strongly, by *not* delegating, you may be depriving someone else of the opportunity to do what they love! Don't be *that* person!

By *not* delegating, you may be depriving someone else of the opportunity to do what they love!

Seriously, though, this is a big shift in thinking for a lot of people. If you have trouble accepting it, look at your Unique Ability activities and think about how you would feel if someone were struggling along incompetently with something that was your Unique Ability and refusing to delegate it to you. Wouldn't you want to say, "Give it to me! I want to do it!" or be dying to literally or figuratively wrestle it out of their hands and just do it the way you know it could be done?

For example, Nicole Pitcher, Shannon Waller's Support Partner (aka Executive Assistant), loves scheduling. (In fact, Shannon often introduces her as her "Scheduling Ninja"!) For Nicole, it's a way to calm down when she's feeling overwhelmed or when there's a lot going on. For Shannon, scheduling itself is overwhelming and makes her cringe. Each of them really enjoys working with the other because their strengths and talents are so complementary. Together they can accomplish far more than either one of them could alone. They determine that Shannon's productivity has doubled, if not tripled, since they started working together. However, until someone like Nicole showed up, with both a passion and skill for scheduling, Shannon had a hard time delegating it. (To compare their Unique Abilities, check out the Appendices.) The point is worth driving home because guilt can shut you down and cut you off from looking for creative solutions. There's a big difference between understanding that you're creating an opportunity for someone versus believing that you're making your problem someone else's. If you've ever passed something off to someone who hated doing it, they simply weren't the right person. Find the right person and you'll both be grateful.

The confines of societal expectations.
Many women struggle with guilt about not enjoying certain activities associated with running a home or certain aspects of parenting (for example, grocery shopping, preparing lunches, etc.). Some men struggle with the stereotype that they should be "handy" when they have no interest in or capability with tools. By acknowledging that it's okay not to like these activities and give yourself permission to delegate them, you'll be a happier partner and parent.

One of our clients who happens to hate mowing the lawn but also felt the pressure to keep his yard looking as groomed as his neighbors', finally gathered the courage to ask his neighbor if he would be interested in mowing his lawn too. The neighbor jumped at the offer and said, "I was wondering if you'd mind if I did it!" Problem solved.

"It would be nice, but … "
Another common thought is, "Sure, it would be nice to stop doing some of these things, but they need to get done!" And you may be right.

There are times when you can't just stop and say, "But that's not my Unique Ability." Nor do you want to use this as an excuse for not doing things others are relying on you for (trust us, that doesn't go over well). The fact is, there are times in life when we just need to be willing to roll up our sleeves and do some things that need to be done, even if they're not "our thing."

However, when facing these less-than-desirable tasks, you do have the choice to do them grudgingly, or be easier on yourself with the knowledge that this is a temporary situation you're working on and that at some point you won't have to do this anymore. Who knows, you may even find a way to incorporate more of your Unique Ability into the task to make it more fun. You're much more likely to get into this creative mindset if you're not feeling resentful or resigned. It's not a tragedy or a failure to be doing something that's not your Unique Ability—only an opportunity for improvement.

How can you grow your Unique Ability?

Now that we've talked about getting rid of what doesn't excite you, let's turn for a moment to how you can do more of what does. As you get ready to do the next exercise, look at the Unique Ability activities listed in your Snapshot. What has to happen for you to increase the time you spend doing these? How can you use them to create more value for others? Are there different audiences you want to work with? Are there improvements or next steps related to some of these activities? If you had more time to spend on them, what would you do? Are there Unique Ability activities on your "wish list" that you'd like to do if you had the time?

Don't be afraid to spend some time focusing your thoughts on envisioning what those activities could become. It will fuel your excitement for what you're most passionate about. The more clearly you can see and feel the benefits of growing your Unique Ability activities, the more compelling it will be to take action on reducing your other activities. This creates a magnetic pull to draw you toward your best life.

If you opted to start with The Naming Path and you happen to have your Unique Ability Statement written, you might want to look at it and consider if there are ways to apply it more in an area of your life where it's being neglected. For instance, you may be able to change your role at work to one that takes more advantage of your Unique Ability. You may be able to find more ways to use your Unique Ability with friends and family or in your community.

One of our clients, Scott Cohen, discovered that his Unique Ability that he applies in his business also worked to help his eldest daughter deal with the "mean kids" at school. Scott's ability to see the facts, quickly cut to the core of a situation, and motivate without sugar-coating the truth to help others know what to do, helped him guide his daughter to make short work of a situation that plagues many parents and kids.

His approach to navigating the issue of girls being mean to one another with his daughter was to go over the entire list of 87 kids in her grade—they spent six hours on a Saturday together—and ask his daughter what she thought of each kid. It turned out there were two girls who were not nice. And, cutting to the core, he said, "You know what, honey? These girls just may not like you. You may annoy them. It's natural to want to be around people, but be around the people that want to be around *you*." And she said, "I never thought about it that way."

In his direct but caring way, he went on to clarify the situation further: "Yeah, it's not about you. They're not saying they don't like you because you're *you*; they just don't *like* you. And not everybody can like you. There are people who don't like me, and they don't want to be around me."

With this new perspective, she went to school that Monday with a changed attitude. She had a clearer view of the reality and what she could do about it. Her report back to him that evening was, "It was easy for me to be around those people. I realized that they just don't like me and that's okay. Now they're *nicer* to me!" And Scott explained, "Yeah, because you *know* they don't really like you, so there's no threat! You're not trying to be someone's friend who doesn't want to be your friend."

Scott's Unique Ability is quickly cutting to the core, providing 100% clarity on what actions to take, and assuredly reaching sound concluding decisions so that people see the light and know what to do.

Scott used his Unique Ability to help his daughter immediately see what she needed to see in a positive way so she could be the best she could be in a difficult situation. He was direct, but caring and motivating, speaking from his own clarity on the issue and telling her directly what she needed to know to take action. When his wife asked, "How did you figure that out?" he said, "I'm a guy, and we don't hang around people that don't want to be around us. We just don't do that." On seeing the facts as they went through the list of students, he was able to see clearly what was not being done the right way, just as he does with his clients and team members in work situations. From there, he was able to empower his daughter to do the the right thing.

Genius evolves from focusing on one thing—your Unique Ability ...

Scott's ability to read people and situations quickly works just as well whether he's at home helping his family, being chairman of a not-for-profit, or running his successful business. If you find you're using your Unique Ability effectively at home but not at work, you might want to look to see if there's a different opportunity to make money doing these activities. By taking a fresh look at how you contribute, you can be happier and create enormous value for others.

Betty Schlacter was using her talents for solving problems and organizing people for years, starting as a little girl on the playground. Later, as a stay-at-home mom and the wife of a jewelry store owner in Peoria, Illinois, she had the opportunity and freedom to hone these valuable skills. As a woman who had grown up in an era and environment where girls were told about all the things they couldn't do because they weren't "suitable for women" (including playing basketball, running, and going to law school), she did what she could with her abilities in the world she had inherited. Her leadership skills were put to use creating solutions for problems that arose in her kids' lives. She thought all this initiative was normal until one of her husband's business associates told her that it wasn't.

Fate thrust Betty into putting these skills and instincts to work in the business world when her husband took his own life, leaving her to take on a failing business while grieving and taking care of her family. Using everything that came naturally to her and that she'd been practicing for years without thinking much of it, Betty, with the help of her son Bob and others, brought that business up to speed. In doing this, she discovered she was a natural CEO, capable of making tough decisions and leading a team through difficult times. Many in her situation would have given up or looked for an easier path. Says Betty, in an excerpt from her forthcoming book (at this writing, a work in progress), "I'm not a Harvard graduate with a business degree. I was a stay-at-home mom with a teaching certificate and a Master's in counseling who faced down tragedy. I learned that by discovering the talents inherent in me, I could achieve more than I ever thought possible."

Less is more.

In our experience, expanding Unique Ability is often a function of zeroing in on a few key aspects of your life that you do enjoy, and eliminating many other aspects that you don't. As you specialize and shave away or shed the non-energizing parts, you find more and more room to learn, grow, and create even more value. Paradoxically, it's by doing fewer things (but at a higher level) that we have the biggest impact and can make the biggest difference.

This is where the most multi-talented individuals are often at a disadvantage. When Dan Sullivan hears someone say, "I can do anything." His question most often is, "Yes, but can you do just *one* thing?" Genius evolves from focusing on one thing—your Unique Ability (which includes several dimensions)—in a concentrated and deliberate way over many years.

In Lewis Schiff's book, *Business Brilliant*, he talks about the ultra-rich and the seven best practices that lead to wealth. When asked the question, "Do you know what you're exceptionally good at that makes you money?" 97.3 percent of the ultra-rich knew the answer versus 54.6 percent of the middle class. In terms of the actual number of skills they had in answer to this question, the ultra-rich had only 1.9 versus 5.5 for the middle class. Bottom line, the very successful are not very well-rounded! They double down on what they do best.

One step at a time.

Before we move on to creating an action plan to make your life better, a few words on expectations: It's perfectly normal to have a flood of thoughts and questions going through your mind at this point. Some improvements may be glaringly obvious and simple, while others seem impossibly complex to fathom. Don't worry if you can't see how to make all the changes you'd like to right away. No matter how resourceful or resource-rich you are, getting rid of non-Unique Ability activities takes time. The goal is to work toward increasing the percentage of time you spend in your Unique Ability—and you will get there!

Think of this as a lifetime process where progress happens in steps, sometimes big, sometimes small. As you go along, you'll see that even the tiniest steps you take toward Unique Ability can have a huge impact on how you experience your life. Getting in motion, no matter how small the first step, is the key.

Focus on what you can change, not what you can't change yet. We've watched many people make small improvements with profound results they couldn't have imagined until they experienced them. Over time, just having your Unique Ability in mind will start to alter your decisions and actions. You can make better choices about what to take on and what to say no to, decide to begin doing things in a way that's more consistent with your Unique Ability, and choose circumstances and relationships that support you in doing more of your Unique Ability activities. All these things represent progress, and if you do this Snapshot again in six months or a year, you'll be able to see how much things have changed.

Right now, we want to get you started on a simple action plan. Give yourself permission to let go of some of your non-Unique Ability activities. If need be, you can come up with a solution whereby these activities still get done—you just might not be the one doing them. Start shifting your thinking from "I have to do x" to "x has to get done."

23 **Notebook Exercise A.3: The Unique Ability Action Plan.**

Now that your mind is swirling with thoughts around what to do, let's create a plan of action.

A. Improvement Ideas.
This is where you get creative and resourceful. Brainstorm and jot down some small changes you could make to eliminate one or more of your non-Unique Ability activities and free yourself up to spend more time working in your Unique Ability. If you're really motivated and see the value of freeing yourself up, you'll find a way to make things happen. Even if you don't know how you're going to do it yet, stay with the idea that it will be possible someday. Your job is to figure out how and when to make it happen. You may be surprised at the ideas and opportunities that come up once you bring this into your consciousness as a goal.

B. Benefits.
To motivate yourself to take action, describe the benefit of making each improvement. You're essentially selling yourself here on why the improvement idea is a good one. Take the time to think this through so your brain registers why you're really doing this. Under Benefits, write how each improvement could make things better. Would this free up your time?

Reduce frustration or stress? Create work for someone else? Add to revenue or profit at work? Would this improvement give your talent new outlets? Make you a happier person? Make the benefits compelling so you're really motivated to make it happen! If you're not sold, you won't do whatever it takes to make a shift.

C. Specific Actions.
Under Specific Actions, list the specific things you can do to make each improvement idea a reality. Use action words and phrases like "call," "meet with," "strategize," "talk to," "ask," and so on. Think of others who could help you out and add them in to this step. Don't be shy about initiating conversations with others around this. Explain your goals and you might be surprised by how much support you receive.

The Unique Ability® Action Plan

	Improvement Idea	Benefit	Specific Action	Deadline
1	Work: Delegate all scheduling & filing to my assistant	- Eliminate errors - Free up my time - Job done better	Schedule meeting & discuss how I can stay out of it all	Next week
2	Work: Ask my assistant to filter my emails so I only see crucial ones	- Free up time - More energy - Better results	Create criteria for which email I need to see	Next week
3	Work: Stop doing new-hire training – switch	- Better training - Opportunity for	Set up time to train Alex & have him	3 weeks

D. Deadline Dates.
In this column, enter a "by when" date for making this improvement. Having a completion date to shoot for helps focus your thinking and actions. Keep in mind all of the other things you've got going on in life so you can give yourself something realistic to aim for. You can always adjust your deadlines if you need to. Copy the deadlines for your various improvement ideas into your calendar to stay on track.

As you brainstorm possible improvement ideas, remember that they don't have to be big or difficult. Even slight changes can be tremendously rewarding when you find yourself free of a task you always hated doing or find that what you most love to do really is valuable to other people.

We often labor needlessly, for whatever reason, thinking that things can't be this easy. Imagine that they can be. Lots of people get to do what they love and get paid for it because they've worked out the fit between their abilities and other people's needs. You can do this too. Even if it's a lifelong process, it makes that life better all along the way. As Dan Sullivan says, "You're going to put in the time anyway … "

"The most valuable thing I took away from going through the process was formulating actionable steps to focus more on my Unique Ability."

Curt Anliker

If you haven't already, go to the Notebook and fill in your Action Plan.

THE BOTTOM LINE:

- Start shaving away your Incompetent and Competent activities first. Stop doing it, delegate it, swap it, automate it, or transform it.
- Excellent activities can take up a lot of time. Work on freeing yourself from these next.
- Don't assume others dislike doing the same things you do. Ditch the guilt and delegate to someone with the right-fit Unique Ability.
- Add at least one improvement idea that expands the use of your Unique Ability, set a realistic deadline, and look for ways to use it in all areas of your life.
- Remember, it's all about "progress, not perfection." Each step in the process represents an improvement.

Moving Forward: Mind Your Mind.

By now you're probably starting to see that Unique Ability is much more than just a tool or a set of exercises. It's a whole different way of seeing human capability and how that can play out in the world. Don't be surprised if you start to notice differences in how you think compared with other people. It can take some time to adjust to this new perspective, and we've seen people get confused at this point, so here are a few quick pointers on how to stay focused, avoid some common pitfalls and unproductive thinking patterns, and accelerate your progress. You can think of these as good "mental hygiene" tips for living a Unique Ability-based life.

1. Don't let "shoulds" box you in.

Many of us have thoughts such as, *"I should do x because [insert your reason or justification here]."* We have expectations that we *need* to *be* or *do* something because the activity is part of our role in our profession, or as a mother, father, community leader, or whatever position we identify with. Or we feel that by not doing this, we will somehow be letting ourselves or others down.

Do we really need to live up to some externally created idea of who we "should" be? Is it true that you need to do things the way others do them or the way they've always been done, or the way everyone in your industry does them? We say no. It's not that things like supporting your family or making ends meet aren't important—they're crucial. It's just that doing them in a way that's true to who you are allows you to grow the best parts of yourself and will be better for everyone in the long run.

Give yourself permission to explore the possibility of creating your own personalized way of doing things, or "role," based on your Unique Ability, that goes beyond being a mom, dad, student, worker, entrepreneur, or professional. You may even want to come up with your own name for it.

Try not to get discouraged if it doesn't feel easy. You may be threatening a long-held sense of personal identity, which requires significant shifts in how you see yourself and how others see you. Even if you're fully sold on the benefits, sometimes others won't want you to change. But if you don't do it, who will? And, if you get amazing results and are more productive than ever, who can argue? You may even start a new trend.

Those who do this inspire others around them to rethink how they're doing things. When people see how much happier and more energized you are, they'll start to ask, "Why do you look so happy? What are you up to?" This is a big part of what happens with our successful entrepreneurial clients as they take more and more control over their own lives.

Reclaiming this command and self-responsibility is incredibly liberating and motivating. Once you make the commitment to focus on your Unique Ability, it often takes courage to challenge the status quo and create your own unique way of doing things. Take comfort in the knowledge that it will get easier with practice and the encouragement that comes with seeing results. Confidence will develop out of that initial courage, once you see that you really can do this, and give you increasing forward momentum. Eventually, the new way becomes normal, and you realize that you have a new capability.

"Before going through The Unique Ability Discovery Process, I kept trying to be someone I'm not. I was trying really hard, but no matter what, I could never succeed. Now, I feel free to be who I really am. Before, I kept thinking, 'I should get better at project managing, organizing, or paperwork,' but now I've got the rationale to let go of that and focus on my unique talents for solving problems, connecting deeply with people, and figuring out what's possible to make things better for everyone. It's hugely liberating."

Phil Caravaggio

2. Recognize that everyone sees the world in their own way.

As you go through your Action Plan and think of improvements that will allow you to spend more time in your Unique Ability, keep this in mind: Each person sees the world through their own eyes. You've had your own life experiences, and you bring with you your own unique talents and passions. Everyone in the whole world has a different—a unique—viewpoint.

We may get frustrated that others can't see or do what we do naturally. (Have you ever said to yourself, "What's wrong with that person? Why can't they see or do x? It's so obvious and easy!") However, this is actually great news. This means that there's a place for each of us to make our own unique contribution. It means that what's a dreadfully difficult and stressful activity for you can be energizing and exciting to someone else, and vice versa. As the saying goes, "One person's trash is another's treasure."

We've met with so many people with diverse interests and talents that we *know* there are people who like, even love, to do those things you find yourself needing to get done that aren't your Unique Ability (right down to tasks like cleaning the fridge!). The more you begin to see and value others' Unique Abilities and unique experiences, the more you'll be open to recognize how different Unique Abilities can strengthen and support one another. Don't be surprised if you start seeing Unique Ability everywhere once you become aware of it. You'll be better equipped to see how you can contribute to others and how others can contribute to you.

3. Commit to proactively increase your time spent in Unique Ability.

Getting rid of non-Unique Ability activities allows you to disengage your mind and emotions from things that don't really get you excited and that actually drain your energy. This creates more time and mental energy to devote to those things you love. To take full advantage of these reclaimed personal resources, make a commitment and proactively plan to use the time and energy you gain to focus more on your Unique Ability. It's not enough to free up the time; you need to take actual steps to develop your Unique Ability with that newfound time. Otherwise, it's possible that you might get rid of one form of "stuff" only to replace it with another. The first step to doing this is to really want to.

> "Unique Ability has made me so much more confident in the person that I am. It really has changed me. I'm such a planner, and that is a big part of my Unique Ability. And now I'm fine with that. It's a bit like being at peace with myself, really, and I'm constantly just trying to strengthen it more and more."
>
> **Andrea Dempsey**

4. Think in terms of investment, not cost.

Ideally, the rewards from making the improvements you've listed should more than make up for any expenses associated with them. Any money you use to hire someone or buy technology to get rid of a non-Unique Ability activity should be considered an investment, not a cost. It's an investment in the future growth of your Unique Ability, which should pay large dividends. In business, the payoff can often be measured in actual future income. Focusing on growing your Unique Ability and using it to create value for the right audience is the best investment you can make in your future happiness and prosperity.

> "At home, I used to hate going shopping, and we've found that we can have our groceries delivered after ordering them online, so we invest the few dollars to do that. I haven't set foot in a supermarket now for three months, and it's fantastic."
>
> **Bob Muller**

THE BOTTOM LINE:

- Watch out for the word "should." Focus on doing more of your Unique Ability activities instead.
- Get rid of energy-draining activities and use your newly freed-up time to focus more on what you love doing.
- Think of your Unique Ability as an investment in your future happiness and prosperity.

The One-Year Goal

Now that you have your Unique Ability Action Plan, let's do a quick thinking exercise that looks at your future in the short term: Look back at the percentage of time you spend using your Unique Ability in both your work and personal life right now. Now think about what your life would be like if you could increase those numbers. If at work, say, it's five percent now, how would your life be different if you were able to double it to ten percent? Remember, this means that not only would you be spending twice as much time doing what you love, you'd be getting rid of activities that aren't your Unique Ability that currently use up that time. Maybe you'd like to increase it even more?

Reshaping your life.
Any increase in the amount of time you spend using your Unique Ability will noticeably improve your life because you'll be replacing activities for which you have no passion with things that give you energy and generate great results. Once you get started, you'll find it easier to identify even more areas where you can do this. You'll develop a much stronger understanding of what your Unique Ability is and how it's best delivered to the world. These are things you can only learn through experience.

Stripping away non-Unique Ability activities is the first step on this path. Michelangelo once said, "The more the marble wastes, the more the statue grows." As the sculptor of your own life, you must systematically chisel away all the extra "marble" that obscures who you really are. Then, the unique work of art your life can be will emerge with increasing clarity. Every layer of non-Unique Ability activity you remove gets you a little bit clearer on what your Unique Ability is and how to do more of it. The energy and benefits you get fuel this transformation and become powerful motivation to find ways to focus even more on what you love.

The indispensable role of others.

Even though your Unique Ability is intrinsic to who you are as an individual, working with others is necessary to achieve the greatest results. The only way to effectively spend large amounts of time in your Unique Ability is to partner with others. Dan Sullivan, after over 30 years of focusing on his Unique Ability, estimates that he spends 95 percent of his work time on Unique Ability activities. The Unique Ability® Team that both he and Babs have worked to build around them is what makes this possible.

Often it's other people's questions and actions that provoke you to spend more time doing your Unique Ability. In the story about Babs and Dan that we told earlier, Babs could see so clearly that Dan was doing things that were obviously not his Unique Ability—and then found other ways to get them done. Dan willingly let activities go and readily acknowledged his talent or lack thereof. His lack of resistance to this process freed him up to apply his Unique Ability more strategically to coaching and developing The Strategic Coach Program. Without Babs's vision of the bigger impact that Dan's ideas could have on the world and her ability to create a support system to leverage him, Dan might still be functioning as a "rugged individualist," trying to do it all himself. Instead, Dan and Babs together have created a company that supports and depends on the Unique Abilities of over 100 team members and creates positive transformations in the lives of tens of thousands of entrepreneurs—many more than Dan could ever have reached as an individual.

Double benefit.

Even when Dan was still doing many things that were not his Unique Ability, the time he did spend focusing on it allowed the company to grow exponentially. There is a double benefit in that much of what Dan gave up was delegated to others who had Unique Ability talents that complemented his own. Not only was his ability leveraged—other tasks were able to take on new life in the hands of people with passion and creativity in those areas. In this way, every percent that was delegated had an exponential return in terms of increased results.

Scott Cohen, whom we met earlier, also estimates his time spent in Unique Ability at work as almost 95 percent. It's been a nine-year process to get there, but it's all been worth it. Others we interviewed were thrilled to be spending even 25 percent of their time in their businesses working in their Unique Ability. While every one of these people has a goal to increase that percentage, they all reported that they felt considerably liberated and energized by what they had already achieved.

28 Notebook Exercise A.4: The One-Year Goal.

Having a goal to work toward is always motivating. To have that "mental push" working for you, set a one-year goal to increase the percentage of time you currently work in your Unique Ability—both at work and in your personal life. Write today's date and beside "Current %," write down the percentage you estimate you spend doing Unique Ability activities right now. Write down a goal for how much time you'd like to be spending in your Unique Ability one year from now. Reach-ing this goal will be an experimental process. You may find that small changes make a big difference, or you may find that you have to do more than you initially thought. The important thing is to keep focused on moving forward

Today's Date: ______________________

WORK:	**Current % in Unique Ability**	☐
	One-Year Goal %	☐
PERSONAL:	**Current % in Unique Ability**	☐
	One-Year Goal %	☐

from where you are now, learn as you go, and celebrate your achievements along the way, whether they're big or small.

Enjoy your progress!

By examining all your activities and bringing them more into alignment with your Unique Ability, you've laid the foundation for a bigger, better future. You've done a lot of work so far, and hopefully you've learned more than a few things about yourself. Whenever life is feeling overwhelming and complex, doing an Activity Inventory will help you take the actions to get you moving and focusing on your Unique Ability again. We've provided an extra set of exercises at the end of the Notebook for you.

You may be eager to get to the next stage—digging deeper to define your Unique Ability. Or perhaps you've already begun to make changes and experience the impact, and this is enough for now. Either way, this is a great time to take a moment to acknowledge and celebrate your progress. You've already done more than most people ever do to clarify how you can make your best contribution to others and to your own happiness. The next chapters will show you how to build on this understanding. You'll define and put words to your Unique Ability so you can then use it to shape the life you want based on your best self.

THE BOTTOM LINE:

- Set a reasonable goal for increasing the percentage of time spent in your Unique Ability, both personally and professionally.
- Commit to reshaping your life around your Unique Ability, little by little. Imagine the difference even a small increase would make!
- Partnering with others who have talents in different areas than yours will be key to your success.
- Each activity you let go of means a possible opportunity for someone else.
- Keep moving forward and celebrate your achievements, big or small, along the way.

4.

The Naming Path

The Naming Path

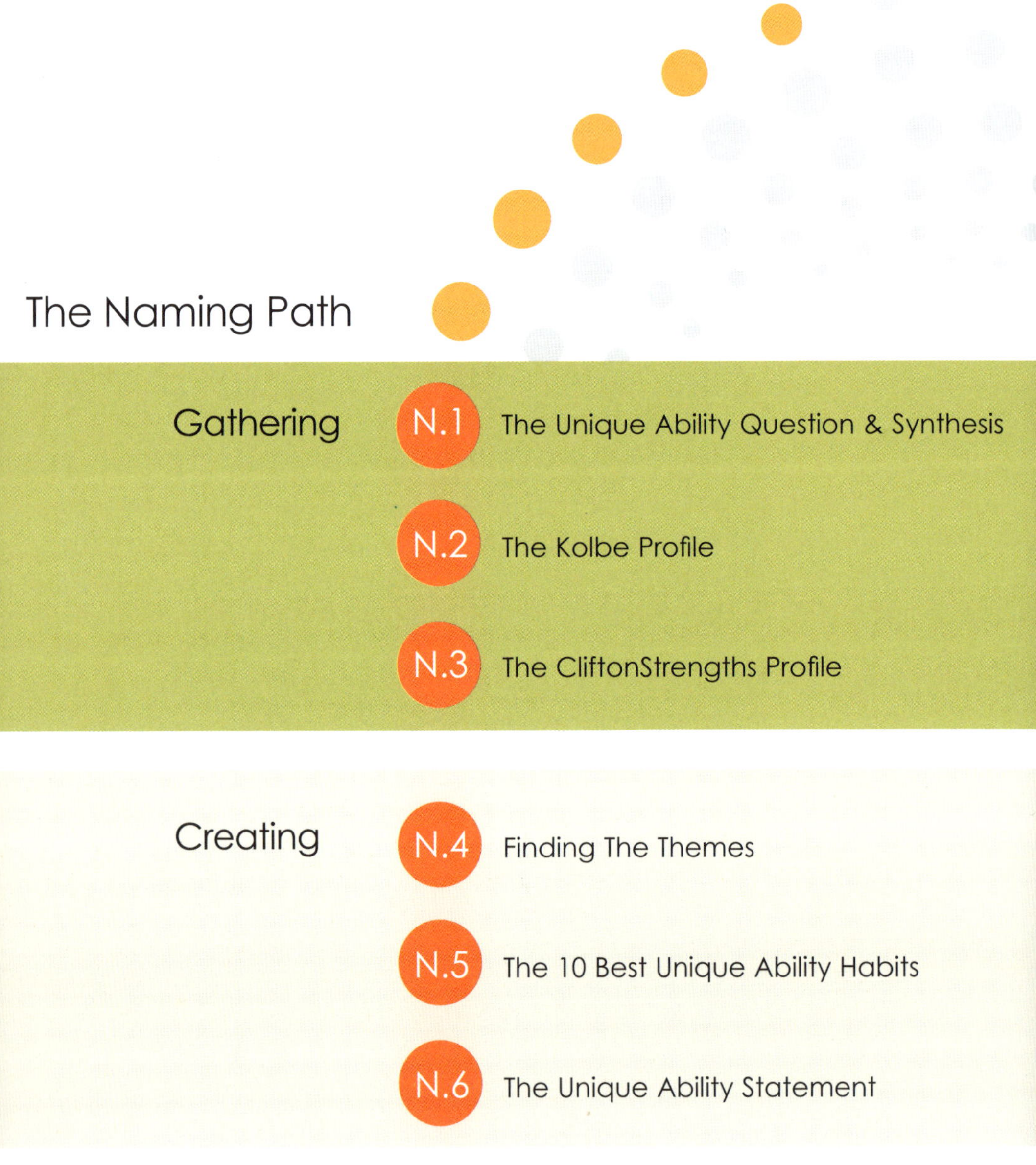

Chapter 4

The Naming Path

"He who names the game owns the game."

Dan Sullivan

Self-discovery 101.
The following pages will take you on a deep and revealing journey of self-discovery that begins by gathering input that you'll use to create and name your Unique Ability. By the end of the Gathering and Creating stages, you'll come up with what we lovingly refer to as "You On A Page." The benefits of this are tremendous and diverse: confidence, clarity, permission to let go, focus, self-knowledge, self-awareness, and appreciation, to name a few. Once you have Unique Ability clarity, you can use it to fulfill the purpose that drove you to pick up this book in the first place. The exercises in this section are labeled N.1-N.6 ("N" for "Naming") to differentiate them from the exercises in The Activities Path section.

Unique Ability shows up everywhere.
Your Unique Ability is the essence of who you are, so it shows up everywhere in your life—at work, with your family, friends, neighbors, and when you're out in your community. Wherever you are, you bring it with you. The exercises we're about to show you will help you gain a much deeper perspective on your unique talents, the results you're most passionate about achieving, what others value about you, how you make a difference out in the world, and what always works for you.

It's at the heart of the activities you love to do and do best. It also reflects the underlying belief systems and all that's behind what the world sees when you're at your best. What are you really doing when you're being uniquely you?

A picture of you.
Going through these exercises, then reviewing and knitting together the results, will give you a picture of yourself that is more comprehensive and objective than what any single tool or measure can provide. The result will likely be more personal and revealing than anything you've seen before. Think of it as weaving a tapestry from many different threads, all of which are uniquely you. This highly personalized picture will allow you to better see how your unique talents and passion might be applied to a wide range of activities and situations. It is also tremendously validating and confidence-building.

The power of naming.
What's so important about putting words around this uniqueness you have, that we each have? Knowing and acting on your Unique Ability is the highest and best use of you. Naming it is a key step in taking ownership of who you are and what you bring to the table in any situation. It allows you to take what you do unconsciously and make it conscious so you can use it even more deliberately.

The benefits of articulating your Unique Ability are numerous:
- **You'll have tremendous clarity.** You'll know exactly what you're good at and the results you're passionate about achieving in life.
- **You'll have a deep sense of knowing yourself.** You'll understand your internal processes—what you're doing every day that makes the biggest difference to others.

- **Your and others' confidence will multiply.** Once you've defined your talents, you'll have a huge boost in confidence. Your own clarity and confidence will in turn give others even more confidence in you and in your abilities.
- **You'll be able to communicate your abilities quickly and easily.** The ease with which you articulate your talents and what you're passionate about will be impressive to others. There will be no stumbling around for words, just powerful, direct communication.
- **You'll differentiate yourself from others.** If you're looking for a job, promoting yourself, or trying to distinguish yourself from others, naming your Unique Ability will help you convey your value in a highly effective way that sets you apart in the marketplace.
- **You'll get a huge boost in self-awareness.** Now that you know what to look for, you'll immediately tune in to new ways to use your Unique Ability and start catching yourself using it all over the place.
- **You'll be better at finding and attracting new opportunities**. It's a whole new radar system for opportunities. With your clear understanding, you'll see and attract the best kinds of opportunities that match your talents and your ability to make a difference.
- **Others will find it easier to refer you.** If you're looking to make connections with people or to extend your reach, others will be more clear on what you can do and will find it easier to share about you.
- **You'll be poised to make much bigger contributions.** Your Unique Ability is how you create the most value for others. It's your unique gift with which to make a difference. If your goal is to make a contribution, you'll be able to contribute far more with greater ease by tapping into your natural abilities.

What to expect: simple but not easy.
Naming, defining, and committing to devote more time to using your Unique Ability is the beginning of a lifelong process of refinement and revelation. Though most of the steps in the following process are simple, for most people it doesn't feel easy. Be sure to cut yourself a little slack. After all, you're a complex, multi-faceted person distilling who you are and what you're all about on one page!

> "It's a tough process, but it's the most rewarding thing I've ever done in business. It's just so liberating to say, 'It's okay to be me. If this is the way I can operate, if this is what I'm good at, if this is how I can add value to my business, to my family, to society, then why am I letting a rule book dictate what I do rather than let my talents and abilities dictate what I do?'"
>
> **Bob Muller**

Immediately upon starting down this Naming Path, you'll see some benefits. As you spend more time using your Unique Ability and have a greater awareness of when you're using it (and when you're not, which becomes really obvious and almost intolerable!), you'll get even better at describing it. Your words will become increasingly precise and refined. You'll start to find new ways to apply it. This sense of continual refinement is completely normal.

At this stage, you're going from "not really knowing" to "having a good idea," which will, if you keep working on it, give way to "getting it really dialed in." Every time your awareness evolves, you'll have more direction, more confidence, and new insights into your Unique Ability and how to apply it to improve your life. Your understanding will continue to deepen over time and with experience, bringing even greater rewards, clarity, and satisfaction.

Aim for a solid first draft.
Once again, the goal in doing these exercises is progress, not perfection. This process will get you a first draft or set of drafts—something for you to try out, refine, and build upon from here forward. We aim for the first 80 percent. The first time you go through the exercises, you'll build a foundation of insight that will open doors to greater self-knowledge and an understanding of some practical changes you can make to start operating more in your Unique Ability. As time passes, your greater awareness will likely lead you to refine your definition of your Unique Ability. You may come up with new or better words, add elements that you hadn't noticed before, or do more wordsmithing that has it sound and feel even more like you. Likewise, as your activities change, you'll benefit greatly from redoing the exercises in The Activities Path section. As a result of all of this, you'll continually be making strides toward working in your Unique Ability more and more, step by step.

Our Unique Ability as your coaches.
As your personal guides and coaches, it's our Unique Ability to lay out the steps and walk you through them. Having guided many different kinds of people through this process over the past 20-plus years, we can attest that if you do the work, the results will undoubtedly follow, and you'll also have many useful insights about yourself along the way.

We've included a lot of coaching here to help you connect with your talents and express them honestly as an "accurate" reflection of who you are. As people who love and appreciate talents, we've designed the questions and exercises to maximize your clarity and understanding of your own unique set of talents. We'll also help you connect with your most meaningful purpose in life. By the end, you'll have a stable and solid foundation for your own personal and professional growth, and a new way to think about your future success.

Despite the big and important subject matter, think of this as a casual conversation, just saying things as they are. As much as we can through these pages, we'll be your "thinking coaches," who will ask you questions so you can have conversations with yourself (and others) about your Unique Ability and how it plays out in the world.

Now, imagine how good it will feel to have your Unique Ability laid out in front of you in one statement. The result is exhilarating, and the journey to get there is so personal and applicable you can't lose. Be open, trust the process, and have fun getting to know yourself better! You won't regret it.

In their own words, here are a few of the effects that naming their Unique Ability has had on some of our clients:

"I am excited and I feel free!"

Bob Woolsey

"It was gratifying and invigorating ... it helped me define on paper who I am. When I showed the finished product to my wife and team members, they all told me it defined me with 100% clarity."

Scott Cohen

"I have a deeper understanding of what makes me tick. Not only did I come away with a clear sense of my personal strengths in my daily life, I also developed a much greater, deeper understanding of my 'true essence' as a person."

Henry Laughlin

"Picture an explosion of vivid color, energy, and noise: My passion is now awakened and I can purposefully use it and share it with all. My family, loved ones, and clients get the best of me when I am in my Unique Ability space."

Chris Wren

"Knowing my Unique Ability gives me the permission, confidence, and clarity to refocus and re-architect my strategies to be more productive and happier. It provided a renewed excitement to actually document these things and build some 'laws' or 'rules' to use as a framework. It's a checks-and-balances system to help me develop a means to hold myself accountable to being the person I am and most want to be."

Jason Friedman

"... Unique Ability has provided me with a sense of permission to just go forward and say, 'This is what I do best,' 'This is where I feel most comfortable,' or 'This is the way I can provide the best direction for what I do for my company, for myself, for my employees, and for my clients.'"

John C. Panter

"As an entrepreneur, the clarity is priceless."

Dave Zumpano

"This process will help you narrow down all of the noise and clarify what truly drives you. I now have a clear understanding of my true Unique Ability."

Jennifer Lincicum

THE BOTTOM LINE:

- Naming your Unique Ability will give you clarity, confidence, and appreciation for your own set of talents.
- It's a tough process to distill who you are and what you're all about down to one page, but the benefits are immediate and liberating.
- Aim for a first 80 percent—just get something down on paper to start, and then keep refining it.
- Trust the process—it works. Go at your own pace, and have fun learning about yourself!

The Unique Ability® Question & Synthesis

Enough about me. What do you think about me?
Because your Unique Ability is so difficult to see for yourself, the easiest way to begin to understand and describe it is to start with other people's perspectives. Hence, the first step of the Naming Process is to collect some input on your Unique Ability from others to use as raw material. For this we use a simple exercise called The Unique Ability® Question.

The principle behind it is this: People who know you well have a certain experience of being with you, and each will have a sense of your special talents. Through their observations, you'll see from the outside what you have difficulty seeing from the inside. The Unique Ability Question takes the form of an email (sample text to follow) that you send to a minimum of eight to ten people you trust, inviting them to give you feedback about how they see your Unique Ability.

You may be thinking, "Wait a minute, you're asking me to do what? Send a letter asking people to tell me about all of the good things about me? Really? That would feel really strange!" That's a very common response, even from the most confident, accomplished people we know.

True, this is not a typical thing to do. In our society, we're not conditioned to ask about the good things about ourselves.

... if we don't know what we're doing that's working, how can we do more of it?

Such activity is often denigrated as "bolstering our own egos," "tooting our own horns," or "fishing for compliments." Self-deprecation, on the other hand, is considered a virtue.

If you value being "well-rounded," you may also believe it's more useful to improve what you're not so good at rather than focus on getting better at what you already do well and enjoy. As a result, the focus is often on problems and areas of improvement rather than what's actually working.

However, there's real benefit in asking for positive feedback. The fundamental premise on which the concept of Unique Ability is based is to focus on your strengths and eliminate or delegate your weaknesses as much as possible. It may feel like a risk asking people what they appreciate and value about you, but if we don't know what we're doing that's working, how can we do more of it?

If someone you care about asked you to do this for them, you'd likely be more than willing to help them out. In fact, you'd probably be glad to have an opportunity to tell them all the things you appreciate about them. It's a bit sad that, often, the only time we get to sing someone's praises like this is either at their wedding or their funeral—and one of those is definitely too late!

Be afraid and ask anyway.
Nonetheless, some people still get tripped up at this point by thoughts like: "What if they don't value anything about me and they feel like they have to make something up?" or "What if I don't like what they say?" or "It feels uncomfortable asking for so much praise."

The fact is, you may not get responses from every single person you ask, but the usual reason is that they just didn't have time to pull their thoughts together by your deadline. People tend to take this kind of request seriously, and they want to carefully consider what they say. More often than not, they're more than happy, even honored, to do this for you. It's very satisfying to tell someone what you appreciate about them in a safe, appropriate context.

"The question really got the process going for me. Reading those replies showed me that my Unique Ability was real, not just something I was making up."

Hamish MacDonald

So, we urge you, even if you're feeling a bit of apprehension, *Do not skip this step!* This is crucial and invaluable raw material for articulating your Unique Ability. There's something incredibly powerful about reading what others think about you—what they see as your unique talents, the characteristics that describe you, what they count on you for. When you see these in black and white, it's easier to grasp that things you do that seem "normal" or "commonplace" to you are actually *very special* to those around you. From there, you can begin to see the big picture of the impact you have in a very personal and heartfelt way.

In fact, even if you were to go no further in naming your Unique Ability, it would be worth doing this one exercise. You'll be touched by people's responses, and they'll be grateful for having had the opportunity to share their insights and perspectives with you. In our experience, for many of those who were reluctant at first, this step ended up being their favorite, and most of those who've gone through the process will continue to hold on to their letters for years to come.

> "When you hear it clearly articulated from the people you most respect, you'll never forget it. You can't un-ring the bell."

Phil Caravaggio

Notebook Exercise N.1: The Unique Ability Question.

Send your version of the following question as an email letter to a minimum of eight to ten people who know you well and whose opinions you respect. These people can be a mix of friends, family members, colleagues, clients, teachers, students, sports teammates, mentors, and classmates—anyone who has been in a position to see you demonstrate your abilities over time.

Feel free to paraphrase or edit the letter so it sounds like you. You may want to be more or less formal or personal or change the wording. Just don't omit the essential question: "What do you see as my Unique Ability?" It's also important to provide a time frame in your letter, as tasks without deadlines have a way of slipping down—and off—people's to-do lists.

Here are two examples to refer to when writing your own Unique Ability Question:

> **Dear Suzanne,**
>
> **I'm currently reading a book about a concept called Unique Ability. This concept is based on the idea that everyone possesses a combination of talents, interests, and capabilities unique to that individual.**
> **I'd really appreciate it if you would help me identify my own Unique Ability by considering the following question**

and sending me back an answer: "What do you see as my Unique Ability?" My Unique Ability includes my talents and abilities, characteristics that describe me, what I'm good at, how I do things, what you count on me for, and any other distinguishing features you see about who I am.

I'd be very grateful if you could respond within the next two weeks if you're interested in helping me. Thanks for your support. I look forward to hearing from you.

All the best,
Frances

Hi Joe,

I have what might seem like an unusual favor to ask you. I'm reading a book about a concept called Unique Ability. It's based on the idea that each of us has a unique set of talents, interests, and capabilities that we're passionate about, and that can be used to create a lot of value for the people around us.

I'm trying to find out what mine is. Because I value your opinion, I was wondering if you could think about this question and send me back an answer: "What do you see as my Unique Ability?" My Unique Ability includes my talents and abilities, characteristics that describe me, what I'm good at, how I do things, what you count on me for, and any other distinguishing features you see about who I am.

It would really help me out if you could get back to me in the next two weeks with any thoughts you might have on this. Thanks so much.

Cheers,
Chris

Take it all in.
Once you've received the responses to your Unique Ability Question, read them through and enjoy what people said. Most people are not used to reading so many good things about themselves, especially all at once! Take some time to let it sink in. This exercise will show you in a very concrete way how your strengths and talents are perceived and valued by those around you. You can keep your letters in the front pocket of your Notebook for future reference.

Notebook Exercise N.1: The Unique Ability Synthesis.

To get an overview of what people said about you and your Unique Ability, summarize the main points of each letter in your

The Unique Ability® Question & Synthesis

Name: S.B. (wife)	**Name:** C. J (biz partner)	**Name:** R. W. (friend)
- strong work ethic	- hard worker, goal-setter	- willingness to take risks
- kind, fun relationships	- tenacity — obstacles	- use props to show ideas
- strong, persistent	- courageous	- ask great questions
- good at fixing things	- great sense of humor	- pull pranks, fun, witty
- love learning & improving	- strong value system	- focused, determined
Name: P. L. (client)	**MY SYNTHESIS**	**Name:** J. T. (client)
- see people's potential	**1.** ambitious, hard worker	- innovative ideas
- high standards	**2.** visionary, future-focused	- think outside the box
- confident	**3.** curious, like to learn	- embrace change
- high achiever, persevere	**4.** tenacious, resilient	- ambitious, bold

Notebook. Then choose the top five points that resonate most with you and write them in the My Synthesis box in the center.

It's validating to find out what others appreciate about you. You'll likely see lots of parallels from people in all areas of your life. You may even discover that the things they most value are not what you expected. Remember, the purpose is to give you a source of raw material to mine for clues. Other people's words and insights will help you get clearer on how you make a difference using your Unique Ability, even if you can't see it. They're the people you're creating value for, and value creation is always in the eye of the beholder.

"The feedback that I got was very useful and insightful, and it gave people a chance to really think about and express who they see me to be and what they appreciate about me. The parallels in the responses were startling."

Dave Pijuan-Nomura

Be respectful and honor people's feedback.
Here we caution you to resist any temptation you may have to downplay or trivialize what's said in the letters. People have been known to dismiss others' observations about them as "personality characteristics," "soft skills," "fluff", "clichés" or otherwise seemingly common attributes. What we've learned is that what may seem like unimportant, mundane, or obvious characteristics are actually incredibly valuable clues that describe key parts of your Unique Ability. Some people truly have a Unique Ability that is centered on relationship-building, making people laugh, communicating, or being loyal and trustworthy—and they create incredible results, both personally and in the marketplace. *Everything* that makes you who you are is significant.

Another possibility is that you may be thinking these results aren't important because they come so naturally. This goes back to our Unique Ability blindness. You think everyone, or at least a lot of people, can do those same things, but in reality, they can't, at least not just like you. It's worth repeating that you're the only one on this planet like you, with your unique combination of talents, reasons for doing what you do, life experiences, and ways of being. As we get further along in this process, the other exercises will help you refine your understanding of how you do these things in a way that's uniquely your own. For now, trust that more will be revealed as you dig a bit deeper. Try to suspend your critical mind and honor people's feedback. Give them credit for the perspective they have from being on the receiving end of your contribution.

When it comes to our own Unique Ability, we're often the last to really get it. We're too close to it. It's so instinctive and comes so naturally that we're oblivious to its power and effect on others. Let your audience be the judge!

"I'm not the one who stated what my Unique Ability is. It came from colleagues, friends, and family. That was the enlightening part: These people from different realms of my life all said the same thing."

Katherine Roberts

A thank-you gesture.

After getting their letters back, many people have taken the time to return the favor by writing back to those people who took the time to respond to their Unique Ability Question. This is a gracious way to say "thank you," and you'll also start others in your life thinking about their Unique Ability in a whole new way. We highly recommend paying it forward and giving the gift of Unique Ability feedback. You will touch many people in the process.

THE BOTTOM LINE:

- Email eight to ten people in your life whose opinions you respect and ask what they value and appreciate about you.
- Even if it feels uncomfortable, do not skip this step! This outside perspective is important raw material for the next steps.
- Once you have the responses, take it all in. Honor what they say as being valid; don't dismiss or downplay it.
- Summarize each response so you have an overview of the key themes.
- Boil everything down to the five points that are mentioned most often and/or resonate most.

Two Powerful Shortcut Tools To Understand Your Unique Ability

Once you've reflected on your Unique Ability letters, you can put them aside. We'll come back to them after we've finished the next two steps. Next in your journey of self-discovery, we're going to gather more fascinating external input using two psychometric profiles that measure your *striving instincts* and your *strengths*. These particular systems we're introducing you to are indispensable for helping people understand their Unique Ability. They're powerful shortcuts that give you more precise language to describe your unique set of talents. They are:

The Kolbe A Index* (created by Kolbe Corp)
kolbe.com

The CliftonStrengths† assessment (created by Gallup, Inc.)
gallupstrengthscenter.com

Each measures something very different. Kolbe measures something called *conation*—your striving instincts, whereas CliftonStrengths is a personality assessment that measures your top five strengths. Each requires that you answer a series of questions online that takes about 20 to 40 minutes to complete. You'll end up with two easy-to-understand profiles that will provide more insight into how you go about achieving successful results in all areas of your life.

It's very important to keep in mind that both of these tools measure only strengths—there are no wrong answers or "bad" results. They aren't "tests" and you can't fail.

Though a small monetary investment is required for each, we feel it's incredibly worthwhile to give yourself the benefit of understanding both sets of results. In our coaching sessions, we would never go through the process without them! It would simply be too hard to narrow down your unique way of doing things and your potential strengths. They define your talents in a simple and relevant way, and provide useful thinking frameworks for understanding how your strengths and talents differ from others'. They're also incredibly useful in helping give you the words to express who you are and how you do things. And, last, they provide tremendously self-affirming insight into important aspects of your uniqueness and how you make your best contributions to the world. Most people find the self-knowledge and context they provide tremendously liberating.

To be clear, we don't benefit in any way financially from these companies. Our motive for recommending them is none other than the fact that they are so incredibly useful in helping to quickly get a description of your best talents. We use them consistently with great success and share them with all our clients and friends because they're so aligned with our belief in maximizing your natural strengths to get the greatest results.

Afraid of being "boxed in"?

Occasionally, we come across "conscientious objectors" who don't like doing profiles of any kind. The objection is usually around the issue of feeling pigeon-holed, stereotyped, otherwise boxed-in or boiled down to something less than the complex and unique person they are. If this is you, we want to assure you that neither Kolbe nor CliftonStrengths pretends at any point to be the measure of you as a person. They are simply providing an outside perspective on certain aspects of how you operate that may provide some new insights. It's like looking in the mirror. It simply reflects back an image, but what you choose to think about that image or how you use the information you glean from it is your choice.

While there are countless profiling tools out there, we certainly don't find all of them to be equally useful in this context. The Kolbe Index and CliftonStrengths are the two we've found to be extraordinarily useful over the years because they provide a simple language and context for understanding our behaviors and choices. One of the biggest benefits that people report is a greater sense of tolerance, acceptance, and freedom as they become even more aware that we all have different ways of doing and being that make a contribution in different ways. You don't have to share your results with anyone else (and risk judgment if that's your concern), and as we've said, there are no "bad" or "wrong" Kolbe or CliftonStrengths results, so there's nothing to fear in using them as learning tools.

The Kolbe Index.

"Success is the freedom to be yourself."

Kathy Kolbe

Go now and complete your Kolbe A™ Index at kolbe.com.

The Kolbe A Index will give you a greater understanding of how a very important part of your mind works that you may not even know exists. Psychological researchers have identified three parts of the human mind: the cognitive part, which has to do with knowledge and intellect (often measured by IQ tests); the affective part, which has to do with feelings, emotions, values, and personality (often measured by personality tests); and the less-known conative part, which governs our striving instincts—how we problem-solve and take action. It's important to look at all three parts of the mind—intellect, personality, and conation. We're going to start with the often-overlooked conative assessment of your own unique way of taking action.

Measuring how you get things done.
The Kolbe Index (kolbe.com) measures your striving instincts. These are an important factor in your behavior, in the mental energy you have for certain tasks, and in how you approach these tasks. Your instincts are "hard-wired" (in other words, you're born with them) and remain constant throughout your lifetime. Knowing what they are will help you understand how

you operate in the world and how you differ from others with dissimilar striving instincts. When you act in alignment with your instincts, you'll find that you have almost inexhaustible energy, whereas acting against them, your energy gets depleted quickly.

> "We have a total commitment to helping people identify, articulate, and use their Unique Ability, and I believe Kolbe does the quickest job of getting you into the right place to start that inquiry—and takes away a lot of the complexity."
>
> **Dan Sullivan**

Kolbe Strengths™.
The report you receive after completing the online questionnaire identifies your instinctive talent and tells you

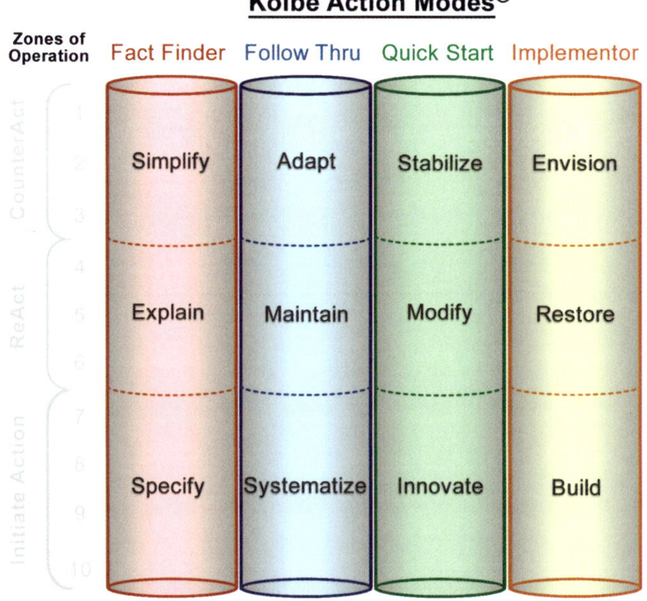

how to put it to its best use. It also provides you with some specific words that describe how you get things done when you're free to be yourself. The four Action Modes** described by the Index are Fact Finder, Follow Thru, Quick Start, and Implementor:

- **Fact Finder** behavior relates to the way we gather and share information.
- **Follow Thru** behavior deals with the way we organize and design.
- We use **Quick Start** behavior to deal with risk and uncertainty.
- The **Implementor** mode relates to the way we handle space and tangible solutions.

These Action Modes determine how you will, won't, and are willing to take action, based on the needs of your instinctive makeup. Kathy Kolbe has done brain research to prove that this is how you *need* to do things to be productive—it's not a "nice thing to have" or something you "want." Doing things using our natural conative strengths allows us to do our best, most efficient, and most creative work.

The 12 Kolbe Strengths.**
Your Kolbe results are charted on a scale from 1 to 10, with each number representing a particular strength. Based on these results, you'll be given four words out of a possible 12 that describe your "Kolbe Strengths"—your approach to problem-solving based on how you prevent problems, how you respond to problems, and how you initiate solutions in each of the four Action Modes. You'll use your four words as part of your raw material for understanding your Unique Ability.

** Action Modes® and 12 Kolbe Strengths™ are trademarks of Kathy Kolbe and Kolbe Corp. All rights reserved. Used with permission.

A source of energy.
This extra perspective will be very helpful when you're looking for patterns in the responses to your Unique Ability Question. It's very likely that you'll see some connection between your instinctive creativity as identified by Kolbe and what people see as your Unique Ability. Since using your Unique Ability gives you energy, as does working with your instincts, you'll find that the two are linked. It's worthwhile to note, though, that passion, which is another source of the energy you get from using your Unique Ability, comes from the affective part of the brain, and so is not part of your conative instincts. But when the two act in concert, it's no surprise that you feel your Unique Ability is actually generating more energy than it's using up.

Digest your Kolbe results.
If you're following our process, you're now looking at your Kolbe results. Take some time to read through them, listen to the accompanying audio where Kathy Kolbe walks you through your results, and look to see how it all applies in your life. You may find this to be a real "aha" moment. Or you may not see its relevance immediately or even question whether it's true. As with the Unique Ability Question responses, let your results sink in and be open to what you're learning.

If you've answered the questions following Kolbe's instructions, "if free to be myself," the profile will be an accurate representation of your natural striving instincts. If you have an asterisk on one or more of the colored bars, this shows that you are in transition: You've either answered the questions inconsistently because you're feeling pulled in a few different directions, or because you're going through an actual transition in life (moving, having a baby, shifting jobs, retiring, and so on). If so, don't panic! At any one time, about ten percent of the population is in transition, and you'll be able to redo the profile (at no extra cost) when things settle down.

> “The day I got my Kolbe results (2 2 10 4) will always stand out in my mind as one of the most powerful days of my life, because that profile suddenly explained where all the troubles in my life and my business came from. I knew from experience that when I stayed within a small circle of activities, I was always most productive, energized, and successful. Yet, I always felt compelled to try to be good at things outside that circle. Kolbe gave me permission to let myself live entirely within my small circle—and for more than 20 years, that’s what I’ve done.”
>
> **Dan Sullivan**

Notebook Exercise N.2: The Kolbe A Index.

Go to your Notebook and record your Kolbe numbers in the boxes at the bottom of the page and circle your four Kolbe Strengths on the graph. Then complete the accompanying short exercise to capture your insights while they’re still fresh in your mind.

More proof that everyone out there isn’t “just like me.”
Besides what you learn about yourself, a useful by-product of completing your Kolbe Index is seeing that other people do things differently than you do. Looking at your results, you’ll see that there are many other possible combinations of striving instincts where people operate either slightly or completely differently than you do.

One of our clients even admitted that before doing the Kolbe, he used to think, “Everyone is just like me, only not as good!” We still get a good chuckle out of that.

In fact, many marriages might have been saved and relationships salvaged if people had understood their Kolbe differences instead of thinking that their partners were doing things just to annoy them! Once you understand and appreciate your own way of striving and see it in relation to the overall landscape of Kolbe possibilities, you'll naturally have a better appreciation of other people's ways. This helps you be more tolerant and appreciative. What might appear to be an annoyance or a weakness is actually just a different kind of strength.

Permission to do things your own way.
One of the greatest benefits of the Kolbe Index is to give you permission to be yourself and to do things your way. When Dan Sullivan received his results, he experienced a huge breakthrough in realizing that it was actually okay for him to make decisions quickly with very little information, to create shortcuts, and to innovate on the fly. In fact, it validated that this was actually the *best* way for him to do things. It also gave him direction about the types of situations that didn't make the best use of his talents.

Keep in mind that your Kolbe instincts don't kick in if you're not interested or engaged in something. For example, if you "Initiate" in Fact Finder (your result is a 7-10) but you're not interested in cars, you're likely not going to research cars or not read the manual. Kolbe has many nuances, but if you get familiar with your profile and allow yourself to do things in your own natural way, you'll be amazed by the jump in your level of self-awareness. We encourage you to check out Appendix A and kolbe.com for more resources, including Kolbe profiles for youth, relationships, and careers, to make use of this powerful tool in all areas of your life. We use Kolbe with all of our team members and clients so we can quickly understand their natural way of doing things and maximize our teamwork and communication.

"After I took the Kolbe A Index and listened to the audio of Kathy Kolbe telling me why I'm special, I made a promise to myself that I was going to help people discover their own greatness. Kathy got me focused on my life's purpose. She helped me realize and appreciate my God-given talent. Now it's my job to spread the word and get people on the track toward their purpose. It's a pay-it-forward sort of thing."

Maureen Sullivan Garrelts

THE BOTTOM LINE:

- The Kolbe A Index measures the conative part of the mind, which governs how we naturally problem-solve and take action. It's not a personality profile.
- You can't fail because it's not a test. There are no "good" or "bad" results.
- Kolbe measures what you "will," "won't," and are "willing to" do when you're getting things done.
- Kolbe describes how you take action in four modes: Fact Finder, Follow Thru, Quick Start, and Implementor.
- Use the four descriptive Kolbe Strengths words as part of your raw material for articulating your Unique Ability.

The CliftonStrengths† Profile.

The CliftonStrengths profile is presented in the book, *StrengthsFinder 2.0*[2] by Tom Rath and online at gallupstrengthscenter.com. This profile identifies a set of 34 possible strengths that the team at Gallup† identified during their research over a 25-year period: "Gallup research proves that people succeed when they focus on what they do best. When they identify their talents and develop them into strengths, people are more productive, perform better, and are more engaged."†† These results are very much aligned with our philosophy of Unique Ability.

By doing your online profile, you can learn your top five strengths. You can also purchase your whole list of 34 strengths if you're curious to see how all of the strengths rank for you (it's pretty interesting to see the top ten and also to find out what's at the bottom). For our purposes, the top five are sufficient.

Go now and find your unique combination of strengths. Either log in online (gallupstrengthscenter.com) and purchase the CliftonStrengths profile, or buy the book *StrengthsFinder 2.0* by Tom Rath and complete the profile using the code included.

††https://www.gallupstrengthscenter.com/store
2 Rath, Tom. *StrengthsFinder 2.0.* New York: Gallup Press, 2007.

Highly engaging, articulate descriptions of the 34 strengths are provided, along with examples of how each strength has been used to create positive results by real people. The words and phrases used in the CliftonStrengths descriptions are great material for helping you understand and articulate key aspects of your Unique Ability.

Bob Woolsey provides a great example as he describes his mom, Betty, whom we introduced earlier. They work together in their family's jewelry business, which Betty took over and ran with no previous experience. Bob remarked about his mom's "Command" strength:

> "I think it gave my mom permission to really go with her Unique Ability and go with what she's feeling because she's spot-on 95 percent of the time. She's a full-blown commander, and there are not a whole lot of those in the world. I think the StrengthsFinder helped her recognize that she is by nature a commander, and she's not going to make everybody feel good and warm and fuzzy (that's where I come in). However, there's definitely a role in life for that person. We probably wouldn't have stormed the beaches of Normandy and had the outcome we did in World War II if it weren't for our commanders."
>
> **Bob Woolsey**

The four domains of leadership strength.
If you want to go further with this, particularly in how it relates to your teamwork with others, check out the book *Strengths Based Leadership*[3] by Tom Rath and Barrie Conchie. In it, they expand the strengths conversation to include the latest research and go further to divide the strengths into four domains:

3 Rath, Tom and Barry Conchie. *Strengths Based Leadership.* New York: Gallup Press, 2008.

The Four Domains of Leadership

Executing	Influencing	Relationship Building	Strategic Thinking
Achiever	Activator	Adaptability	Analytical
Arranger	Command	Developer	Context
Belief	Communication	Connectedness	Futuristic
Consistency	Competition	Empathy	Ideation
Deliberative	Maximizer	Harmony	Input
Discipline	Self-Assurance	Includer	Intellection
Focus	Significance	Individualization	Learner
Responsibility	Woo	Positivity	Strategic
Restorative		Relator	

1. **Executing**—People who "know how to make things happen."
2. **Influencing**—People who "help their team reach a much broader audience" and are "always selling the team's ideas inside and outside the organization."
3. **Relationship Building**—People who are "the essential glue that holds a team together."
4. **Strategic Thinking**—People who "keep us all focused on what could be" and "continually stretch our thinking for the future."

Exercise N.3 Notebook: The CliftonStrengths Profile.

Now you know your Top 5 Strengths! Go to your Notebook and write them down. You'll use these five words to help in identifying and articulating your Unique Ability. Read through the descriptions of each and think of examples of how you might be using them at work, at home, with friends and family, or in your community. Don't worry if you don't see them immediately. They are sometimes still in the realm of "potential strengths" that haven't been fully developed yet.

We've listed other CliftonStrengths resources in Appendix A if you'd like to learn more.

THE BOTTOM LINE:

- The CliftonStrengths profile is a personality assessment that gives you your Top 5 Strengths out of a possible 34.
- The descriptions of your Strengths provide great raw material for helping narrow down and understand your natural abilities.
- Note where your strengths lie in these four domains of leadership: executing, influencing, relationship building, and strategic thinking.
- Use your strengths as themes for articulating your Unique Ability.

Finding The Themes

After enjoying and absorbing the feedback you've received from The Unique Ability Question, the Kolbe Index, and the CliftonStrengths profile, it's time to organize and synthesize all the input you've received. You may find your own way to do this, but we'll share the best way we've found to sift through all this valuable information. The goal is to sort everything into themes, categories, or "buckets." Not everything will fit perfectly, but if you aim for an 80 percent result, you'll find that strong patterns start to emerge. Use what you know about yourself to see what fits where. After you synthesize what you've learned, you're going to come up with your very own "Top 10 List of Talents" based on the most relevant and meaningful categories from all your input.

Go on a "word hunt."

As you do this exercise, imagine you're going on a "word hunt." Articulating your Unique Ability is all about putting words around your particular set of special talents. Other people's words, from your letters and profiles, are the starting point to zero in on the most vital elements of your Unique Ability. And after that, we'll figure out how to talk about what you're doing using *your* words. In the end, you'll be expressing it in a way that's meaningful, feels familiar, and in your own voice. It will sound like you. Starting with the evidence provided by others helps us combat Unique Ability blindness and appreciate our own value as others do.

Notebook Exercise N.4: Finding The Themes.

Go to your Notebook, and we'll help you identify the themes that emerge from everything you've gathered so far.

sample

STRATEGIC COACH®

Finding The Themes

Themes

1. Ambitious, hard worker
   - Achiever strength, passionate, driven
   - strong work ethic, want more
   - high achiever

2. Visionary/future-focused
   - Futuristic strength, future focus
   - visionary leader, inspire others
   - dreamer

3. Curious, learn
   - Learner strength, thirst for knowledge
   - love learning
   - desire to learn

4. Tenacious, resilient
   - strong, persistent
   - tenacity through obstacles
   - focused, determined, not discouraged

Themes

8. Improvise (9 Quick Start on Kolbe)
   - innovative ideas, creative problem-solver
   - think outside the box
   - embrace change, take risks

9. Restore (4 Implementor on Kolbe)
   - good at fixing things
   - use props to demonstrate

10. Maximizer strength
    - love improving, high standards
    - always want better
    - see people's potential/strengths

11. Relator strength
    - kind, loving relationships
    - create relationships
    - caring

THE BOTTOM LINE:

- Using the input you've gathered—The Unique Ability Question, the Kolbe Index, and your CliftonStrengths results—you'll see themes or patterns emerging.
- Absorbing this outside feedback helps combat the Unique Ability "blindness" we all tend to have.
- These themes will provide the foundation for your 10 Best Habits, the detailed description of the ten key elements of your Unique Ability.

The 10 Best Unique Ability® Habits

On the Night You Were Born
By Nancy Tillman

"On the night you were born,
the moon shone with such wonder
that the stars peeked in
to see you
and the night wind whispered,
'Life will never be the same.'
Because there had never been
anyone like you ... ever in the world."[4]

Now that you've got some big building blocks in the themes you just wrote down, we're ready to start putting your Unique Ability into words—your words. There are two parts to this. The first is writing your 10 Best Unique Ability Habits, which are in essence a detailed description of your Unique Ability. After that, we'll use the most meaningful words from these to sum everything up into a one-sentence statement—the bottom-line version of your Unique Ability.

You have the necessary raw material. Now all you need is some time to look behind the curtain and think about what it is that you're *really* doing that generated the feedback in your letters and profiles. This will require you to delve into your own natural, often unconscious behavior in a way that you've probably never thought about before. The questions are simple, but the answers will be new to you. It may be a stretch to find words to describe your talents that you feel

4 From ON THE NIGHT YOU WERE BORN © 1999 by Nancy Tillman. Reprinted by permission of Feiwel and Friends an imprint of Macmillan Children's Publishing Group. All rights reserved.

comfortable with. One client joked that it was like "trying to describe breathing." So don't worry if this part of the process feels a bit challenging. That's totally normal. We're really getting into the nitty-gritty here of defining your Unique Ability.

Expect finding just the right words and the way they fit together to take several drafts. Some people may have something they like after three attempts, whereas others may take as many as 15 before they're happy with the end result, and all of this is fine. It's not easy to be objective about something so close to you, and you have a lot of different dimensions to describe. One important piece of the puzzle—*the passion that drives you*—is usually something you've never even considered before.

Trust the process.

As you work through this thinking, take heart in the fact that, over our many, many years of experience with this process, we've learned that it *always* works. So just trust it and trust yourself, get comfortable, make sure you're free from distractions, and let's get a first draft on paper.

Allow yourself to start with whatever comes to mind. With every draft, you'll make huge improvements. It's okay for this to be a work in progress that you go away from and come back to with fresh perspectives over days, weeks, or even months. You may want to do it in stages, taking some time in between, or you may want to go through and do a first draft of all ten and then take a breather. Whatever feels best to you is great.

NEED EXTRA HELP? If you'd like to have someone walk through this exercise with you, don't hesitate. Find someone you feel comfortable with to be your sounding board. The best kind of person for the job is an open-minded, attentive listener. Have them ask you probing questions to get deeper insight into your behavior and write down exactly what you say. This is what we do in our 1:1 coaching sessions. Be clear that your aim is to describe what you're really doing in your own words. Also, sharing your drafts with others who know you well to get their input can be tremendously helpful. They may say, "That's so totally you!" or they may ask great questions to help you get clearer with your wording or more insightful in your understanding. Do whatever makes the process easiest for you.

Your unique set of "habits."
We call the framework we use to organize and define the key parts of your Unique Ability your "10 Best Unique Ability Habits." By our definition, these are the things you always do *automatically* and *naturally* to produce your best results, which is why we call them habits.

We use the word "*always*" with a caveat. It doesn't mean every single second of every day, *rather this is how you operate when you're at your best, and being your true self.*

You've developed these habits over the course of your lifetime, and depending on what stage of life you're in, you may have already made lots of progress—and will continue to make even more in these areas.

Once you put yourself in a position to see it, you'll realize that you have a real feel for using your Unique Ability. It's created lots of visible results in your life. People, like those you got your letters back from, recognize it in action. Keep in mind that we're not talking about life or health habits, like exercising, flossing your teeth, or eating ten fruits and vegetables (not that those aren't good ideas!). We're talking about how you naturally use your talents and strengths to do good for others out in the world.

Here are a few snippets of real people's Habits to give you a sense of what they can look like. Yours, of course, will be unique to you.

Phil Caravaggio

Me At My Best Headline	What I Always Do And Why
1 Vision of best	I believe that the boundaries for what's possible can always be pushed beyond where people think, and always think about how I can make things better in order to foster real confidence and growth.
2 Integrity & vulnerability	I try to remember who I actually am and what I actually feel, know, don't know, and think, and hold that in mind in order to create a deep connection and to create an invitation for others to be the same. "Remember who you are."
3 Pursue clarity of thought	I look through the haze of a situation and see its essence, logic, and assumptions to find out what matters most and to solve the core problem.

Charlene Poitras

Me At My Best Headline	What I Always Do And Why
1 Generating energy	I generate a joyful exchange of energy that leaves people feeling more positive.
2 Heartfelt listening	I listen to people and take their words to heart so they feel heard and appreciated.
3 Space for honesty	I connect with people emotionally, create a safe space where they can sit in the moment of truth, and then offer a stepping stone.

Tasha W. Thomas

Me At My Best Headline	What I Always Do And Why
1 Growth Facilitator	I listen for the underlying authentic motivation, and then illustrate using examples and comparisons to support people in uncovering their next steps for growth.
2 Connect Through Imagination	I engage in in-depth conversations where I explain, vividly describe, discuss, share ideas, reenact, and tell stories in order to create and deepen my connections with people.
3 The Goddess Factor	I honor and share who I am by genuinely expressing my opinions, beliefs, and desires.

"When good skills become habits, we lose awareness of them and their amazing value. The Unique Ability Discovery Process reminds us to use them more often and improve them."

Frank Creaghan

A word on good versus bad habits.
At the mention of habits, the idea of "bad" habits often comes to mind first. If you look more closely, though, we *all* have a set of habits that govern our everyday actions. Whether you consider them "bad" or "good" depends on whether they work for or against the things you're committed to. For this reason, we prefer to think of them as "successful" or "unsuccessful" habits.

In the spirit of focusing on your strengths, we'll highlight the successful habits and leave the unsuccessful ones aside for now. We aim to focus on the successful habits in such a way that the unsuccessful ones get crowded out, delegated, or managed. Inside the spectrum of all your successful habits, you have a smaller set of "best habits." This is where you want to focus so you can magnify what's best about you.

Your own set of working principles.
From all your successful habits, we're going to pull out the top ten. These 10 Best Habits reflect your values; you do these things because they're important to you. In fact, you can't help yourself; you do them because that's how you're wired. Others recognize that you do these things and have likely acknowledged you for them (as you've seen in the answers to The Unique Ability Question). These Habits are not *ideal* behaviors you *wish* you had or think you *should* have; they're the actual set of working principles that show up consistently in your life. It's important to be honest with yourself about this.

The magic behind the curtain.

From doing your Finding The Themes exercise, you now have a list that includes characteristics describing you, your strengths and talents, your way of looking at life, and your way of being. For the most part, these words and descriptions come from external profiles and other people (apart from those you added yourself). In this exercise, we're going to go one level deeper and look at what's underlying each of them that's special and unique to you.

There's a difference between *other people's perceptions and descriptions* of what you're doing and what you're *actually doing* to create the results described in each of these clues. Think of it as a theater production: For everything that happens on the stage that the audience sees, several more carefully orchestrated things are going on backstage to produce that effect. Essentially, we're going to look at the magic behind the curtain and describe what you're "really doing" that has people say these things about you. This is how we'll come up with your 10 Best Habits. By taking what's unconscious and making it conscious, you can give your best actions room to grow and flourish.

> "My Unique Ability Statement really hit me as the true me, the one I was looking for."
>
> **Jean-Pierre Blanchet**

Ginger Price, a very successful cosmetic dentist and entrepreneur, was interested to see "good people skills" and variations of it—like "always in a good mood" and "great bedside manner"—come up in every Unique Ability letter she got back. These "soft skills" were highly valued by everyone she had asked. After delving a little deeper, it became clear that there are some very specific things Ginger does that create these impressions, and they're not quite what you might think. The great bedside manner that people were experiencing was the tip of a much bigger, multidimensional iceberg that looks like this:

> **Strategic.** I see things as a fun game and constantly develop strategies. I think and act strategically—all of my actions have a bigger goal.
>
> **Positive.** I wake up happy. I'm very conscious of setting the vibe around me, so wherever I am, it's a happy place to be. This allows things to get done easily, with no muss, no fuss, while at the same time focusing on the best in each other and expecting the best.
>
> **Woo.** I strategically ask questions to find out what people want; listen with interest, curiosity, patience, and without being attached to the outcome; let them unravel; match where they're going; get them in the problem with me; let them be in charge; try to enlighten them along the way; and then reflect the strategy back to them in a way that wins them over and makes it easier for everyone.

Who wouldn't feel that a dentist or boss who operated in such a way had great people skills? Only Ginger could identify what she really does, though, to have people feel this way.

What does a Unique Ability Habit look like?

As you're trying to describe your Unique Ability Habits, see if what you're thinking meets the following characteristics. If so, you're on to something good. You can also use the following checklist to help spur your creativity. These are the clues that your Unique Ability is switched on:

Checklist: The Characteristics Of Unique Ability

- **Superior skill:** Others would agree you're really good at this. You'll likely have evidence to support this from your letters and from the profiles you completed.
- **Passion:** You really enjoy doing this and are passionate about it.
- **Energy:** It gives you energy and energizes others when you do it.
- **Never-ending improvement:** You keep getting better and better at it.
- **"Factory-installed":** To some degree, you've been doing things this way since you were a kid (ask your parents, siblings, or teachers if possible). Maybe you weren't as aware back then or it wasn't developed yet, but these habits have been part of you since you were very young.
- **Feels totally natural:** The characteristics that are a key part of you (for example, your sense of humor and fun, the fact that you keep your word, your ability to research, your "jump right in" approach) are all part of your Unique Ability.
- **Feels easy:** What you do may not seem exciting or special because it comes so easily to you. Others may recognize it in you before you see it yourself. In fact, you may even find yourself frustrated or irritated when others don't act in this way. You assume it's so easy or obvious that others can do it too (which is most often not true).
- **Meaningful and important:** You consider these actions to be very important, you value them, and they feel incredibly meaningful to you.

- **Underlying essence:** Unique Ability is at the heart of the activities you most love to do and do best. It's the set of underlying actions, belief systems, and ways of being, thinking, doing, or seeing the world that are unique to you. You then apply these to various activities in life.

- **The "best" way:** You see this as the "best" way to operate. It would feel wrong to do it any other way—it just wouldn't be "you." You can't understand why everyone doesn't do it this way too because it works so well.

- **Creates the most value:** This is really how you best create value for all the people in your life—your family members, friends, clients, prospects, students, or colleagues at work. It might be what you get paid for, or not.

- **You're a hero:** You may not think of it this way, but in some sense you're being a "hero" to others in these areas—people can always count on you to do these things, which impacts them in a positive and useful way.

- **Consistent:** You act this way consistently in all areas of your life when you're being your best, true self.

- **Multiplies results:** This is the way for you to truly expand the impact you have in the world, be the most productive, and create the greatest results.

- **Constantly evolving:** The understanding, description, and application of your Unique Ability is a constant work-in-progress. Your self-awareness will increase the more you use it in different situations and with different audiences. Over time, who you are as a person won't fundamentally change, but your Unique Ability will evolve throughout your life and will keep getting better the more you apply it.

These are all clues that you've found a great Unique Ability Habit! Any Habit that exhibits these characteristics taps into your talent, your passion, and your values. If you can't truthfully say you always do it and that it comes naturally, then it's probably an ideal behavior you aspire to or just do once in a while, rather than an actual Best Habit.

> "It was really kind of astounding. I was sometimes in awe of some of the things that were brought out that either I didn't know at all, or that I had really thought were no big deal. There were things that I just didn't really feel were of any particular value, but as I went through the process, I realized they were. It became more normalized. That would be a good way to describe it."
>
> **John C. Panter**

Another good filter is how long you've been doing it. If it's a true component of your Unique Ability, it's likely you've been doing it for many years. You may even have childhood memories of how it shaped your life in some way. Or perhaps you can trace its evolution back to a time when you learned that this way of acting worked for you.

Include both your talent and your passion.
In each Best Habit, there will be two main parts: Unique Ability is, one, *what you do best* (your talent) and, two, *why you love to do it* (your passion). Therefore, in each of your Habits, you're going to write action words that describe what you do, and add words that describe the "why"—the result that drives you to do it. The talent part may have several components, including some description of "how" you do it. You are by definition passionate about taking these actions—there's a fulfilling purpose that propels you. The "why" part describes the value you want to create—the overriding reason behind your behavior

or way of being or doing. If you don't have two parts in each and every Habit, don't worry, but most will.

Unique Ability Habit =
What I do + Why I do it
(talents) (passion)

I always ...
To ground us in the fact that this is a natural, repeated way of doing things for you, we're going to begin with the words "I always ..." This doesn't mean 100 percent of the time, but it really is what you do when you're truly being yourself. We usually take the "always" out later, but for now, use it as a trigger for your thinking.

Writing guidelines.
As you go about writing your Best Habits and then, later, your Unique Ability Statement, use these guidelines to make sure you come up with a great result and have fun along the way:

1. **Use your own words.** You don't need to be a practiced wordsmith—use words you would naturally use in everyday conversation. The words don't have to be fancy or otherworldly. Make sure it sounds like you. If other people's words feel true to you, go ahead and use them. Don't worry about it being poetic or impressive. Its force isn't in the phrasing but in its ability to make you say, "Yes, that is me. That really is what I do. I love doing that. I'm always that way when I'm at my best."

2. **Look for your actions, underlying beliefs, and how you're being.** Look for action words that get to the heart of your superior abilities, like "explain," "connect," "strategize," or

"create." Your Unique Ability may also include the way you're being ("remain calm") or the way you look at people or life or your beliefs ("I believe that the boundaries of what's possible can be pushed" or "I see adversity as opportunity" or "I'm grateful to be alive every day").

3. **Aim for 80 percent.** Don't worry about what you come up with being perfect right off the bat. We're going to create a first draft, and you can tweak it going forward. It may start off sounding awkward, but it will get better. By getting the first layer written down, you'll be able to uncover the next layers. As you keep editing, you'll become more and more clear, and it will become more and more fun!

4. **Write it for yourself.** You are the primary audience for this. These aren't "marketing" statements to be posted on your website or put in a resume (although some have done that). They're written first and foremost for you. You are the primary audience, with a goal for *you* to get clear on your Unique Ability. You can share them with others, but that's secondary, and we'll address that later, so don't worry about what other people would think right now.

5. **Make sure it can be applied to many different situations, activities, and opportunities.** Your Unique Ability will manifest itself in all areas of your life, so make sure you write in such a way that it can be applied everywhere (not just professionally). If you can only think of work examples (that's fine and normal since this is one place where many of us really use our Unique Ability), ask yourself if you do this with your family or friends. Chances are you do. Use the word "people" instead of "client" and see if it holds true. If not, maybe it's not truly part of your Unique Ability. Avoid

business lingo as it automatically narrows the scope.

6. **Be as detailed or as succinct as you'd like.** It can be written simply—in only a few words—or can include a lot of detail. Either is fine. Your Unique Ability will reflect how you normally express things. Each person is different, so do what feels best for you.

7. **Describe both your talent and your passion.** Each element of your Unique Ability has a "what you do" (talent) part of it, combined with a "why you do it" (passion) part. Add in a description of "how" you do it to make it sound more like you.

8. **Your talents are normally integrated and overlap.** In reality, your Habits work together in an integrated way. They aren't really "separate." To clearly understand and define them, we're pulling them apart and writing them as distinct points. Trust your instincts about what fits in each "theme" or Habit. If an idea is covered in one point, you don't need to repeat it elsewhere unless you really feel like you need to.

NEED EXTRA HELP? If you're grappling at all with the thought that these Habits aren't unique, don't focus on the words "Unique Ability." Instead, focus on the thought: "This is what I'm good at and love to do." Start each sentence with: "I love, or I'm energized by ... (insert verbs plus the result you're hoping to accomplish here)."

Choose your top ten themes to describe.
Let's create your 10 Best Unique Ability Habits. Look back at the themes you summarized from all the input you received. From your long list of themes, circle the top ten that stand out as most important to who you are. One by one, we're going to go through your Top 10, and we'll find words to describe the Unique Ability that underlies them. You may end up finding a way to include more ideas by combining some of them, so keep that in mind. To kick off your first draft, you're going to pick a topic or theme that is particularly meaningful to you.

Let's do an example together. Let's say that many people have commented on your curiosity and inquisitiveness. In your letters, people may have said things like "You have a variety of interests, you're a lifelong learner" or "You ask a lot of questions to understand things." You may be the kind of person who takes courses, reads books, seeks out mentors to learn from, explores different cultures, or chooses to continually put yourself in new situations where you're required to learn. On the CliftonStrengths profile, you may have "Learner" in your Top 5 if you love the act of learning itself, or "Input" if you like to gather or collect lots of information that you might need later on.

For each Best Habit, ask yourself: What am I *really* doing that has people say this about me (what verbs best describe this), and *why* am I doing it (what result do I want to accomplish)?

Find the underlying pattern of behavior or way of being.
There's something at the heart of each theme that you're really good at and love doing. You're digging deeper to articulate

what's really going on. This may not be obvious right away. Given the basic question, "What are you really doing and why?", maybe your first draft of your Habit is, "I always learn new things so I can be more resourceful." Notice the "what": "I always learn new things" and the "why": "so I can be more resourceful." This is now your first draft of Habit 1. You're going to edit and do more wordsmithing after you come up with the rest of your Top 10 list. If you feel like you need more than one sentence to properly articulate your Habit, feel free to have more. Many people have expanded their Habits to include many dimensions, and it can be too challenging to fit it all in one sentence.

Jana Mackic has this talent for learning, and after thinking about what she does naturally and why she does it, she describes her Best Habit this way: *"I'm curious and inquisitive, and I find things intriguing. I'm always learning so I can be more resourceful and constantly improving."*

Think of an example or tell a story.

If you need help figuring this out, think back to an example at work, with your family, or in any part of your life where you do this. You're looking for the "underlying process" that you do here and in all situations across your life. Keep thinking of other examples (there will be many) where you do this particular action and look for the pattern of behavior—what you're "always" doing and why you're doing it. Once you start to figure out what you're really doing, ask yourself, "Do I also do this with my family and friends? Do people count on me for this?" to confirm that it truly is a Unique Ability Habit. Refer back to the Checklist: The Characteristics Of Unique Ability for more on this.

"The 10 Best Habits was the most cogent summary of me that I've ever seen. I think it's a greater representation of who I am, what I do, and why than any resume could ever hope to be, and is a great deal more valuable to my relationships than anything I could tell them in a day's conversation."

Marc Sumner-Smith

Add a "headline" to your Habit.

Before we draft all of your Habits, let's do one more thing. As we've revised our process over the years, we've added another component to make them even more useful. We've added short headlines, titles, or sayings that sum up each one. Start with a first draft that sums up the Habit and then improve upon it later. This provides a few things. It's a fun way to get a quick snapshot of your Habits at a glance and an easy way to remind yourself of the key areas of your Unique Ability later. It also gives you an opportunity to incorporate phrases, nicknames, or terms that are relevant to you and are fun or memorable. You can keep it simple with one word or come up with your own catchy title. What's acceptable? In a nutshell, anything! We've had people use terms from TV shows or movies, sayings or mantras that resonate, and we've even had people make up their own words. See our real-life examples for some ideas. Anything goes. As long as it feels authentic to you, go for it! Jana labeled her habit describing her love of learning as "Curious Learner." This summed up the idea best for her.

"The headlines are little mantras that I tell myself. All of those things in my Unique Ability are things I've done all my life, and now I have little verbal cues written down so I can remind myself of who I am."

Phil Caravaggio

10 Best Habits: Examples Of Headlines

Curious
Better and better
Make things fun
Simplify
Respect
Problem-solver
Flying wit
Good judgment
Integrity
Failure's not an option
Storyteller
Junkyard dog resiliency
Extra mile
Supportive
Values
Competition
Wordsmith
Positivity
Spark excitement
Full throttle
Head full of ideas
Focus

Explain
Intuition
See patterns
Simplify
Passionate
Learner
Faith
Explorer
Teacher
Analyze and decide
Strategic
Harmonize
Empathize
Effervescence
Terminator
Skeptical
Eagle's view
Outlandish ambassador
Sensible
Goal achiever
Sponge for experiences
Designer

NEED EXTRA HELP? If you're getting stuck on words, be playful. Get something down on paper to play a bit more with later. Choose words that you would use in daily conversation. Don't worry if they don't feel quite right yet.

Getting below the tip of the iceberg.
Since we all have a tendency toward Unique Ability blindness, it's not unusual to still be thinking, "What I do isn't really unique—a lot of other people can do what I do too." Usually, this is just a sign that you need to dig a little deeper. What you're seeing at first glance is like the tip of an iceberg. It's the most visible part, but what really differentiates us from others is found in the part of the iceberg that's hidden beneath the surface.

Let's look at a few examples where on the surface people's talents look similar, but when you look at what lies beneath, you clearly see the uniqueness. In the broad sense, yes, there are lots of people who are responsible and trustworthy, or who are good at solving problems, or who make people laugh, or who can analyze, or who can come up with new ideas. That's just a first pass at describing a talent. When you look a little deeper, you'll see that your uniqueness lies in the nuances of what you do: how you do it, what you bring from your belief system and past experiences, and why you do it. In this way, you are different from everyone else. Each Habit you have is unique to you. And, on top of that, your combination of Habits is also completely unique to you. No two people in the entire world have exactly the same blend of talents and passion.

To illustrate, we'll look at two common talents that we often see on the lists of our entrepreneurs—A, positive energy and enthusiasm, and, B, problem-solving. How they show up differently for different people will become clear.

Talent A: Positive energy and enthusiasm.
Many entrepreneurs we've met have a natural ability to see the positive. They have an enthusiasm and energy that's contagious and always uplifting, often despite facing big challenges or obstacles that others would see as negative.

They create fun wherever they go. They can turn a negative into a positive very quickly and do so naturally. This can also show up as Positivity on the CliftonStrengths profile.

Here are a few examples of how this "positive energy" can show up uniquely for various people. You'll see that each "what" and "why" is different. People have chosen words unique and meaningful to them. What's meaningful to one person isn't always meaningful to someone else.

> **Make things fun.** I have a positive outlook and share that positivity with people so they laugh and have fun in whatever we're doing together. **Ryan Duffy, Energy Entrepreneur**

> **"Funomenal."** I appreciate each day, and with the attitude of challenging the status quo and enjoying the journey, I treat every day as a blank canvas where I'm the artist. I paint with fun—the essence of being nimble in thought and task so I can flit among the possibilities that are available. **Peter Buckle, Chartered Financial Planner & Entrepreneurial Wealth Manager**

> **Endless and infectious enthusiasm.** I approach everything with an abundance of enthusiasm and positivity and an energetic attitude, which is infectious and motivates people to be enthusiastic about something as well. **Stephanie Pal, Natural Food Entrepreneur**

> **Improvisation.** I'm passionate about all that I do. I'm always playing and improvising in ways that consistently create new opportunities, fun, laughter, efficiency and accomplishment, satisfaction, love, and happiness. **Neil Moore, Pianist, Composer & Founder of Simply Music**

One particularly poignant example of this is that of Jorge Martinez Moyar, who, after witnessing the birth of his baby girl, learned that she had been born with Down Syndrome:

"I remember it like it was yesterday. It's a situation that no one wants to be in. The moment my daughter was born, you could see it, but I didn't have the courage to ask. My wife asked the doctor if she had a chromosomal problem, and the doctor said, 'Yes, she has Down Syndrome.' Immediately, I could clearly see what we were getting into. This gave me a sense of peace. I knew where I was: I was in a situation I couldn't quit. I had to face it. The first words I said to my wife came naturally to me, 'Honey, we're in a great situation. I know these three things are true: One, I'm sure we're going to live at least 120 to 150 years because we cannot abandon her, so we're guaranteed a long life. Two, this is the easiest way to get to Heaven. And three, we're going to have a lot of kisses and hugs, laughter, and joy with her ... for life!' I went to the doctor and asked, 'What do we have to do now?' And he said, 'Nothing ... feed her.' And I thought, okay! So I got the camera and took pictures, like I did for our other three kids. I just switched the situation because defeat and depression were never options. This is a mental exercise that I did naturally to face the situation. It happens to me all the time. That's the way I think."

This is a perfect example of Jorge's resilience, as he describes it here:

Resilient. When faced with a challenge, I always find the opportunity. I mentally choose the positive, face reality, quickly see the blessings, and transform a negative situation into a positive. **Jorge Martinez Moyar, Financial Advisor, loving father & husband**

Talent B: Problem-Solving.
Another example of a component of Unique Ability that shows up a lot in our client base is the ability to solve problems and help others see strategic solutions where they saw only confusion. Entrepreneurs can turn this ability into a business that creates tremendous value for others. It may appear as "Strategic" on the CliftonStrengths profile. Here are some different examples of how the problem-solving ability shows up for people, as articulated in their Best Habits:

> **Resilient strategic adaptor-collaborator.** I always look for possible ways to solve something no matter what the circumstances are. I rethink the situation to find the freedom and growth within the perceived restraints, choose to find a way to do what's needed in a joyful way, and shift my perceptions in order to honor my true commitments. I have a strong will. Nothing can stop me. *"Do I have any choice and freedom in this? Is there a higher and better way?"*
> **Jeff Peoples, Software Entrepreneur**
>
> **Stealth Strategist.** I easily pierce through a situation and think through the steps from a 30,000' perspective; imagine the "if-then" scenarios; look at obstacles, challenges, points of friction, and opportunities; and then map out a clear schematic from start to finish to create the best possible outcome.
> **Yuri Elkaim, *New York Times* Bestselling Author, Health & Fitness Coach**
>
> **Strategic thinker.** I get a feel for how something's working, how it's not working, and where we want it to get to by asking questions or by immersing myself in how things are functioning today. I then see where it's broken or where it could be better, experiment with "what if's," and put things into a format that makes sense of the clutter so I can evaluate and come up with a reasonable path to get to whatever the ultimate goal might be. **Paul VanDuyne, Professional Engineer**

Strategic. I have a strategy behind everything I do and a plan to get where I want to go. I start with the goal, quickly and logically process the problem, analyze different scenarios, see the path of least resistance, and choose the best plan to achieve the result with maximum efficiency, which may include innovating a new solution from scratch.
Jennifer Lincicum, Benefits Advisor

Strategic problem-solver. I see the possible outcomes, either negative or positive, and always choose the positive. I figure out what has to be solved and keep going. I analyze the issue or situation, know that there's a better way, and instinctively predict a way to make the best use of resources, maximize efficiency, and avoid negative outcomes. I then come up with a solution that will change the course of action to the positive. **Martha Rodriguez, M.D., Internal Medicine Physician**

These Best Habits were created after lots of thinking, questioning, and several drafts, so let them inspire you to dig down and really think about the components that are part of what you do naturally. When you put them together and find the words that are meaningful and inspiring to you, you'll start to see your uniqueness come out in words. Let's go to your Notebook and get started.

Notebook Exercise N.5: The 10 Best Unique Ability Habits.

Draft 1: Draft Your Top 10 List.
One by one, go through the top ten themes you circled in your themes list and create a Best Habit for each. Put words around what you're "really doing and why." Get a first 80 percent draft done. Keep going until you have a first draft of all ten. This may take you hours, or you may space it out over a number of days. If it looks like you've got some stray ideas that don't fit into your Top 10, maybe they don't make the cut.

Or, see if you can weave a few ideas together. You'll likely have a good sense of what belongs with what, even though everything overlaps.

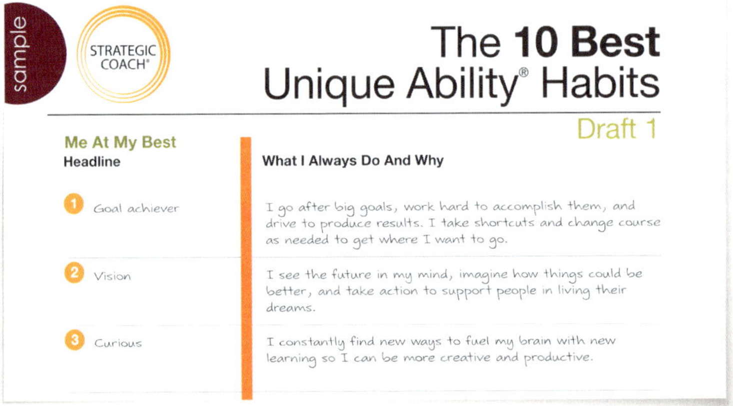

Draft 2: Edit, tweak, revise, add, and move things around. Once you have your first draft of all ten, it's time to take another look at each of them and start the "editing phase." You're going to go through each Habit, one by one, word by word, to see how you can make each one sound better. This might involve looking for different words to express what you're saying (we often use a thesaurus and/or dictionary for ideas), shortening or simplifying, shifting the order of words, or adding important details that are missing. Ask yourself, "Is this what I'm really doing?" "Is there more?"

Your goal is to come up with an accurate and complete picture of how you always do things and why you do them. Dig deep and keep playing with what you've got. Pay attention to how you feel when reading—if you have a feeling of energy and excitement you're on the right track. If not and something seems off, keep working, make a few changes, and do a new draft.

Your description might be plain and simple, or it might be complex and detailed. As long as it reflects who you are, it's great. You might spend a lot of time refining your Best Habits before you finally get something you feel good about. When we do our 1:1 coaching sessions, this step of writing and revising The 10 Best Habits is the most challenging and time-consuming, and often takes several hours of concentrated work, even with an experienced coach. Our brains often hurt by the end, but we come up with a list of Habits that are energizing and meaningful. It's a great feeling, so it's very worthwhile persisting until you get something that feels just right.

Draft 3: Refine and reorder.
After you play around with each Habit individually, feel free to put them in an order that suits you. Some people don't care about order since they all overlap anyhow. Others feel that certain Habits belong first, while others go at the end as an anchor, or that there is a sequence or flow that makes the most sense—almost like your own personal creativity process.

If you feel more comfortable working on a computer than with pen and paper, typing up your Habits might make them easier to edit than doing it by hand in your Notebook, but it's up to you. We usually make changes, type them up, then reread, tweak, and do another draft. We keep at it until we get something that resonates.

An ever-evolving document.
You can expect that your description will evolve over time as your understanding of your Unique Ability grows. As you test your Unique Ability out in the world and have experiences with your newfound self-awareness, you'll find yourself honing it, getting clearer and clearer about the nature of your Unique Ability and how to articulate it. Realize that even the earliest draft will be light years away from what others who haven't

undertaken this challenge have. People generally don't think about themselves as unique, let alone try to define their uniqueness in words. No matter what your words are, you now have an increased awareness of what you do and why you do it. This shift in consciousness can make a huge difference in your life.

Congratulations—you've just come up with the in-depth description of your Unique Ability!

Test your 10 Best Habits on others.
When you're finished editing (for now), you'll have a set of personal principles that guide your everyday actions. To check out the accuracy and truth of what you've come up with, test them out on some people who know you well. A good group of people to test your list with is the group who responded to your Unique Ability Question. Ask if anything is missing. Check to see if they think your Habits "sound like you." They may even be able to help you refine some of your Habits to get at more precise ways of describing what you "always do." In our experience, a person's 10 Best Unique Ability Habits create a recognizable portrait of who they are. In many cases, we can remove the person's name, and friends, family members, or co-workers who know them well can identify the person just from the list of Habits.

George Carras laughs when he remembers how his 15-year-old daughter saw his fourth Habit, *"Communicating Ideas. I express, develop, and vet ideas using visuals, stories, and analogies in honest conversations with trusted others"* and exclaimed, "That's so you, Dad!" That was when he knew it wasn't just about the business, but who he was as a person.

Here are a few more examples of people's 10 Best Habits to illustrate more of the diversity of what's possible when writing your own:

Compete with myself. I create competitions with myself and compare my actions and results to how things were done before. My competitiveness always drives me to be better. **Mitchell Chapman**

Rock the boat in a positive way. I am easygoing, maintain an even keel, stay calm, and provide steady reassurance in order to create a stable environment where everyone feels safe and can see clearly, so we can have the best chance of finding solutions, improving the outcome, or preventing chaos. **Alex Gould**

Remember details. I naturally remember details about people's lives and use them in conversation to make them feel special, remembered, and comfortable. **Kristi Chambers**

Identify potential obstacles. I look for, see, and communicate the potential dangers, obstacles, holes, and problems that need to be considered in order to execute a plan smoothly—with as little backtracking as possible. **Danielle Noga**

Includer. I reach out to the people who seem to be outside the group looking in, and try to connect in order to make them feel welcome and included as part of the team. **Tanja Lee**

THE BOTTOM LINE:

- Your 10 Best Unique Ability Habits describe what you "always" do, naturally and automatically, when you're at your best.
- Each Best Habit will meet certain criteria: You have a superior skill, passion, energy, and a sense of never-ending improvement.
- Go deeper and ask yourself, "What am I really doing that has people say these things about me?"
- There are two main components to each Habit: the "what you do" (your talents) and "why you do it" (the result you're passionate about creating).
- Aim for a first 80 percent draft to start—just get something down on paper. With each draft, you'll get to a more accurate description of your Unique Ability.
- Make sure you can apply each Best Habit to all areas of your life—it's not just about your work.

The Unique Ability® Statement

"The clarity and confidence boost that comes from nailing down your Unique Ability in a single sentence is powerful."

William Ellis

Distilling into one sentence.
You've done the hardest part of this whole process by coming up with ten descriptions of what you do naturally when you're at your best and doing what you love—your 10 Best Habits. Now we're going to boil these down to "you in a single statement." Just to reassure you, most people find this part relatively easy after doing what you've just accomplished.

It's time to extract your Unique Ability Statement—the one sentence that expresses your Unique Ability in a bottom-line way.

This will allow you to express your Unique Ability to yourself and others in a simpler way—one that can more easily be remembered and repeated, which is useful in many circumstances. It might have a lot of dimensions to it, but we're going to figure out "what and why" in a nutshell.

You already have all the right words because you're going to choose words from your Best Habits. The only tricky part is figuring out how they fit together to articulate your Unique Ability. To keep it simple, we're going to use pretty much the same formula you're already familiar with from crafting your

Habits. Then you'll go through a similar editing process to the one you did with the Best Habits until you get a Statement that feels right.

The formula.
The formula for creating a Unique Ability Statement starts with the words "My Unique Ability is … " followed by a set of action words or phrases that describe what you do (your talents), and then words that describe why you do it (your passion).

My Unique Ability is …

my talents + **passion**
(what I do and how I do it) **(why I do it)**

54 **Notebook Exercise N.6: The Unique Ability Statement.**

Circle the key words.
The first step to drafting your Statement is collecting the most relevant key words from the latest draft of your 10 Best Unique Ability Habits. While all of these words are important to you, we want to describe the gist of your Unique Ability, so look for the words that pop out to you as *most* crucial for describing *what* you do and *why*. Circle those "most meaningful" words and write them in your Notebook in the space titled "Key Words." Be discerning. As you work on your Statement, if you find you need more words, you can always go back and grab them.

Draft 1: What I do.
Once you have your list of key words, you're going to start drafting your sentence. Start with the first part—your talents.

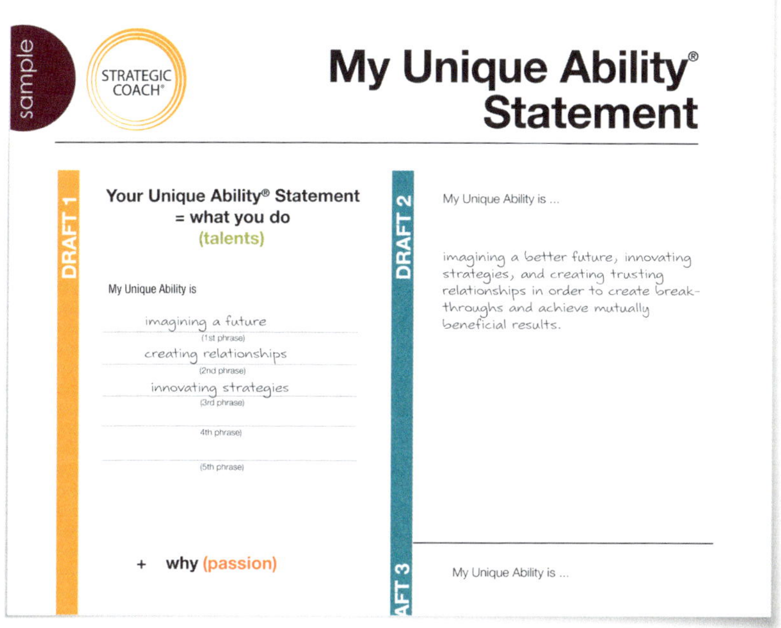

Look at your list of key words and see what fits. Ask yourself, "What do I do first?" or "What's at the heart of what I do?" Usually, there will be something that feels like your starting point, or something that is at the core. You may also want to describe the way in which you do this. Jot this down without worrying about how to make it a sentence. Just get the idea on paper. Then ask yourself, "What comes next?" and find the verbs or phrases to describe that. Do this for each component of your unique set of talents until you feel like it's enough. There will likely be several sections or phrases that make up this first "what" part of your Statement. There are three in our example, but feel free to use as many as you want.

It's akin to figuring out your true purpose in life—it's THAT big.

Remember to only draw on the words from your Best Habits. If you think of new or different words that you like better, go ahead and use them, but then go back and revise your Best Habits to include them. There will be congruence between your Habits and Statement because they articulate the same thing, with one being a summary of the other. You're going to be the judge of how much you're going to include in your Unique Ability Statement. Some like it very detailed, whereas others have a very short and simple sentence. There is something to be said for creating a brief Statement that you can remember and share with others, but make it as comprehensive as you feel necessary.

A few examples of the "what."

As with your Best Habits, it's important to get something down on paper to let your brain engage in the process. For many people, there are multiple dimensions to what they're doing. As an example, "My Unique Ability is analyzing the details and creating logical, focused systems … " Analyzing details and creating systems are both integral parts of this person's Unique Ability. Here are other examples of the "talent" part of a few people's Unique Ability Statements:

Paul VanDuyne
My Unique Ability is envisioning possibilities, thinking strategically, and collaborating in a fully committed manner ...

Andrea Dempsey
My Unique Ability is connecting with people by asking questions and openly sharing in conversation, then organizing and planning ...

> **John C. Panter**
> **My Unique Ability is** observing, asking questions to explore people's opportunities and talents, and compassionately guiding them to think, make decisions, and take action ...

Keep it general.
Notice that these actions can be applied to many different arenas. They have to be, in order to encompass the many circumstances in which you may use your Unique Ability. Unique Ability at its essence is not a profession or career title, nor is it a specific activity, like "selling cars" or "writing books." The direct applications of your Unique Ability to specific situations are really "Unique Ability Activities" that we looked at in The Activities Path.

Finding your "why."
The "why" part of your Unique Ability Statement is a really big deal. It's akin to figuring out your true purpose in life—it's THAT big. You get really clear on what lights you up, what connects with your heart and your true passion. You may not know yet where or how to apply it, but it gets you to the essence of what drives you, the impact you're most compelled to have on the world.

In his highly entertaining commencement address to the class of 2014 at Maharishi University of Management (which you can find in its entirety on YouTube at the time of this writing), actor Jim Carrey speaks eloquently about the importance of the effect you have on others, calling it, "the most valuable currency you have." He then goes on to describe what motivates his work, and it's not what one might think. As you listen to his speech, you begin to see that he's all about bringing comfort and freedom from concern to people, which he learned from his dad. He saw at a young age that he could ease people's suffering by using his comedic talents, which he did for his mother, who was afflicted with a number of illnesses. His desire to have his "why" have an effect on more and more people developed into a successful career as an actor, comedian, and children's book author, and has made him a household name. It's clear that he sees his work as a way of serving those who need it, and that when he realized why he was doing it, his clarity, focus, and effectiveness took a leap forward. Perhaps most important, his love of doing what he does and his delight in the life he gets to live as a result are also abundantly clear. Standing as the example of what can happen when you do, he asks each student in the commencement audience to consider what the world needs that their talents might deliver, what they might love doing in the process—and encourages them to imagine *big*.

So, let's figure out what that is. Jim and the others we've met in this book have pondered this quite a bit, which puts them at an advantage. Our next task is to get you on that same path so you can live life doing what excites you the most, with the satisfaction that you're making the biggest possible impact on others. That's a life well-lived.

Draft 1: Why I do it.

Once you feel like you have the key parts of the "what" your talents are, move on to the second part of your sentence. The basic question here is, "Why do I do this?" In other words:

- What result are you hoping to achieve?
- What's your motivation?
- Why do you bother?
- What are you really committed to?
- What lights you up?

This part of your Statement describes your passion and the kind of impact you want to have. Sometimes this part of the sentence is easier to come up with than the description of what you're doing. Again, there may be a few components or dimensions to your why. Feel free to make it as long as you need to at first to capture whatever you think is important. You'll have plenty of opportunity to edit and refine it later.

> "The part that I thought was so cool about this process is just figuring out the why. You know you do certain things, but realizing why you do them is really interesting to me. You realize why certain things are important to you. You learn why they're a part of who you are as a person and help you know just how you can better contribute to all situations."
>
> **Jayne Stymiest**

Here are the "why" parts that go along with the people's talents ("what" they do) we shared with you a few pages ago:

Paul VanDuyne
... in order to achieve stretch goals that produce results to be proud of and maximize the outcome.

Andrea Dempsey
... so people feel happy and better about themselves.

John C. Panter
... that will result in them pursuing their life's imagination.

Put these two parts together, and, voila, you've got a basic first draft of your Unique Ability Statement, as you can see here:

Paul VanDuyne
My Unique Ability is envisioning possibilities, thinking strategically, and collaborating in a fully committed manner in order to achieve stretch goals that produce results to be proud of and maximize the outcome.

Andrea Dempsey
My Unique Ability is connecting with people by asking questions and openly sharing in conversation, then organizing and planning so people feel happy and better about themselves.

John C. Panter
My Unique Ability is observing, asking questions to explore people's opportunities and talents, and compassionately guiding them to think, make decisions, and take action that will result in them pursuing their life's imagination.

Drafts 2 and 3: Play around with the words.
Just as you did with your Best Habits, the next stage is all about editing and playing with words to come up with something that feels right. Here are some ideas as you do a few more drafts:

- Read your sentence out loud.
- Go through it word by word and see what fits and what doesn't.
- Try rearranging words—it can make a big difference.
- Read your Statement to others who know you well to see what needs refining.
- Check whether you'd like to add some descriptive words (again, pull from your Best Habits) to complete the picture and personalize it more. These can help describe how you do what you do.

Test the results.
As we've said, it's important to test your sentence to be sure it applies to all the situations in your life where you use your Unique Ability. For example, in addition to your work or school activities, it also needs to apply at home, with friends and family, and in the daily activities where you exhibit a superior ability and passion. Here are a couple of examples of how an effective Statement can be applied to a variety of activities and reveal the common thread through all of them:

Myrna Nemirsky's Unique Ability is "finessing and organizing every detail to create an enjoyable experience that is both impeccable and harmonious." At work, she applies this to her job as a writer, editor, and proofreader. In the editing and proofreading process (including of this book), her goal is to produce a piece that is clear, concise, and easy to read. As the last "pair of eyes" to see everything before it is sent out to print, she makes sure everything's in the right place to create as perfect a piece as possible. However, Myrna's Unique Ability is not just evident in her work life.

At home, her Unique Ability comes out in her passion for cooking, entertaining, decorating, and gardening. In her cooking, as much as she loves the cooking process itself, creating a beautiful experience for her guests is her main motivation—even when those "guests" are her two grown children. Her unerring eye for detail is also reflected in her garden and in her home's charming décor.

Another reflection of her Unique Ability is her dedication to creating a stable and harmonious home for her family. She sees her Unique Ability in action in such everyday activities as doing laundry, writing an "organized" grocery list, and choosing and wrapping a "just right" gift. Friends and family members are always delighted to be on her guest and gift lists—and are rarely, if ever, disappointed.

Remember Chad Johnson's story we shared in Chapter 1? We've included Chad's complete Unique Ability in Appendix B so you can have a closer look at his underlying talents and the results he's most passionate about creating. If you look closely at his Habits, you can see that he's been honing his Unique Ability for his whole life, since he was a kid who inspired his siblings and cousins to create their own circus. That inspiring leadership is a common thread that's shaped his life into a set of unique experiences that make complete sense once you understand it as the underlying theme. Whether it's helping his classmates, building a business through teamwork, or getting his kids to clean up after dinner and learn leadership skills and accountability along the way, Chad has had his best successes and built an incredibly rewarding life by using his Unique Ability to approach life's challenges with fun, energy, and passion.

You can see from Chad's and Myrna's examples that they each use their Unique Ability in a lot of very different activities—activities that might even seem completely unrelated if it were not for the understanding of their Unique Ability. This is normal and one of the great gifts of insight that come with beginning to see Unique Ability, both your own and others'. As you begin to notice Unique Ability, you start to see these connections. When you're able to focus more on using your Unique Ability in all these different areas, and possibly start to see how you've been using it for years as you look back, it brings a tremendous sense of alignment and integrity to your life as a whole. What's common in all these activities you love is *you*. As you do any one of them, you're honing your Unique Ability in ways that are likely to make you better at *all* of them—even if you don't notice right away. Your

Statement will help you find this core of your being so you can consciously sharpen your focus and see how to develop your Unique Ability through the many ways you use it now and the new ways you might use it in the future.

Looking at someone's Unique Ability is like looking at the most beautiful part of them.

> "My biggest insight, aha moment, light bulb suddenly lighting up over my head was finally seeing how my Kolbe, my StrengthsFinder, and all the other pieces that make up my Unique Ability are reflected in everything I do. It's 100%, totally, authentically me."
>
> **Myrna Nemirsky**

58 Notebook: You On A Page.

Now you're ready to pull everything together! To truly have "You On A Page," rewrite your Unique Ability Statement followed by your 10 Best Habits in your Notebook. This page should articulate fairly well who you are, what you do best, how you operate, and essentially what you're all about! Looking at someone's Unique Ability is like looking at the most beautiful part of them. You're looking at your essence—something that has such an incredible impact on all the people around you. It's a big part of what makes you who you are and makes other people gravitate toward you. If you were to share this with others, it alone would give people an excellent idea of what they could expect from you and count on you for.

Now that you've done this thinking, how do you feel?

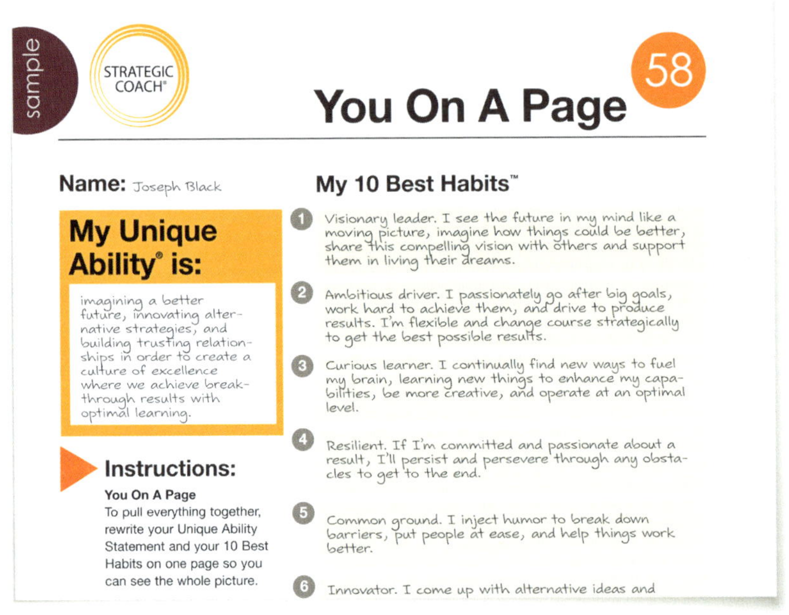
sample

STRATEGIC COACH®

You On A Page 58

Name: Joseph Black

My Unique Ability® is:

imagining a better future, innovating alternative strategies, and building trusting relationships in order to create a culture of excellence where we achieve breakthrough results with optimal learning.

Instructions:

You On A Page
To pull everything together, rewrite your Unique Ability Statement and your 10 Best Habits on one page so you can see the whole picture.

My 10 Best Habits™

1. Visionary leader. I see the future in my mind like a moving picture, imagine how things could be better, share this compelling vision with others and support them in living their dreams.
2. Ambitious driver. I passionately go after big goals, work hard to achieve them, and drive to produce results. I'm flexible and change course strategically to get the best possible results.
3. Curious learner. I continually find new ways to fuel my brain, learning new things to enhance my capabilities, be more creative, and operate at an optimal level.
4. Resilient. If I'm committed and passionate about a result, I'll persist and persevere through any obstacles to get to the end.
5. Common ground. I inject humor to break down barriers, put people at ease, and help things work better.
6. Innovator. I come up with alternative ideas and

Bob Muller, a now reinvigorated Jeep dealer in Australia, had this to say:

> "The thing I got out of going through The Unique Ability Discovery Process was realizing that I was in the right industry doing absolutely the wrong job for 30 years. The job I had passion for and that I was good at was delegated to someone who was less passionate and probably not as gifted as I was. So after going through the process, I went back and totally rearranged the business, and put myself into a job that I just really love. I don't mind going to work now. I used to hate it. I get way greater enjoyment out of my work now. I'm passionate and my ideas are starting to flow."

Stuart Poonawala, the UK-based financial planner we met in Chapter 3 said,

> "Before knowing my Unique Ability, I would always question, 'Why do I want to start a marketing company? Why do I want to set up a coaching company?' I would always be questioning, 'Is my skill set actually being in marketing because I would say, well hang on, I've never worked in marketing, I've never been trained in marketing, and I didn't do a marketing degree. So what gives me the right to say I'm a good marketing executive or designer?' Well, actually my Unique Ability gives me that. And that's the only validation that I need."

Bob Woolsey's positive attitude and Unique Ability fit perfectly into the family jewelry business, but he didn't always know whether he'd chosen the right career. He said,

> "My Unique Ability could go into many different businesses. It's fun to be in the jewelry world, where it's a happy business. The experiences that I'm creating for people are really, truly happy, so it's a great fit for me. I get to help people start their lives on a positive note. My Unique Ability is *'engaging in conversation, listening, recognizing what's going on, and proactively helping people move toward logical action so they can celebrate positive achievements and enjoy a happy life.'*
>
> "Essentially I figure out what people want, talk to them, find out a way to create a solution to whatever they're going through, and move them to a happy ending. It's perfect for what I do. For years I suffered through wondering, 'Should I be in the jewelry business? Am I in it just because it's a family business? Is this really what I

> should be doing?' So it was really awesome to recognize that, 'Wow. I am in a perfect place.' And what else can I do within this place to help others? That was my initial reaction after going through The Unique Ability Discovery Process. Then I came back to the store and immediately got out of things that were not my Unique Ability."

Ben Stellino, a sales consultant and serial entrepreneur, shared,

> "Working in sales, I think clarity about my Unique Ability helps me the most when I'm speaking to prospective clients. It helps to choose the right words to help them feel more comfortable in describing what it is that they're really after. Knowing my Unique Ability has really tweaked my listening skills as well. My Unique Ability includes capturing the moment, living in the moment, listening to what people have to say, being very conscious of my words, earning that trust, and helping people come out of their shell. I think the biggest impact it's had on me is that I have consciously slowed down and pulled back and really listened to what people have to say. It's helped with my confidence and acceptance of what my Unique Ability really is and just playing toward that."

Charlene Poitras, a Strategic Coach team member who coaches our entrepreneurial clients and organizes events in her spare time said it like this:

> "Now that I know what it is, I can bring it to the table at all times. I think before I discovered my Unique Ability Statement, I knew there were times that I just rocked and there were times where I just didn't feel like I was in my groove. Having a really keen distinction between

those different times feels like a chance for me to say, 'How can I be awesome all the time?'"

THE BOTTOM LINE:

- Your Statement is a bottom-line summary of your 10 Best Habits.
- Keep it general enough to fit in a variety of situations, while making sure it has enough detail to sound like you.
- Each word in your Statement comes from the work you've already done and will be meaningful to you.
- You're describing "what you do" and "why you do it," just like you did in the Best Habits.
- Play around with your drafts until you come up with something that feels good—it's exciting, motivating, and inspiring to you.

5.

The Road Ahead

Unique Ability®
2.0

Chapter 5
The Road Ahead

"The secret to a happy life is to discover what you love doing and develop a way of getting paid for it. A greater secret is to do what you love, get paid for it, and make a great contribution to other people. And the greatest secret of all is to do what you love, make a great contribution, and get extraordinarily well paid for it."

Dan Sullivan

Let's stop for a few minutes to take stock.

One great reason to do this is to celebrate your progress—to take a moment to acknowledge what you've already accomplished before we begin to map out what lies ahead. If you've worked your way through the exercises in this book, you've definitely learned a lot and done some pretty powerful thinking. And even if you're still getting started on the actual exercises and have just decided to read ahead, it's likely there are already useful changes taking place in your understanding that are worth observing.

Another reason to reflect is to bring awareness to the way your perspectives may have changed as a result of what you've done so far. As our underlying view of how the world works evolves, and our place in it changes, so do our responses to many things, our values, and even what we choose to give our attention to. In short, you may begin to notice that you feel differently about certain things, people, or situations than you did before. Understanding how this relates to your work on your Unique Ability will help you deal with those changes more consciously and productively.

A new mindset.

The truth is, the world looks different through the lens of Unique Ability. It's a mindset with wide-reaching, life-altering implications. What are you starting to see more clearly that you weren't seeing before? Let's have a look at this now. Here's a recap of some of the most common realizations that begin to sink in for people as they start learning about Unique Ability and observing it in action:

- **Everybody has one.** Now that you've had the opportunity to explore your own Unique Ability, it's probably easier to see how everyone has a Unique Ability, even if they haven't identified or developed it yet. Not everyone necessarily wants to work on or develop theirs, but the potential is there in everyone. By articulating yours and beginning to understand how Unique Ability works in the world, you give yourself a distinct advantage over those who don't have this knowledge. This is partly why people who first go through this process often have a tremendous desire to share the concept with others they care about and want to collaborate with. One of the main reasons we wrote this book was to make this sharing easier.

- **It's the ultimate energy source.** Using your Unique Ability is the most energizing, satisfying, and potentially rewarding way to create value for others. Once you start to recognize and differentiate what it feels like to be working in your Unique Ability versus everything else you do, it often becomes clear how much you're giving up or not tapping into by spending time on non-Unique activities. People's feelings about this vary from frustration and extreme agitation, especially at the beginning, to powerful motivation and excitement around the possibilities for improvement.

- **It feels like freedom.** Getting rid of non-Unique Ability activities and focusing on doing more of the things you love to do and do best is incredibly liberating. Even small changes that shift the balance more toward Unique Ability can relieve huge amounts of stress and fatigue, reduce feelings of being boxed in, and restore a sense of being more in control of your life and your future. Even if you're not actually implementing these changes yet, just identifying what they are allows you to begin to imagine what your life will be like when you do. That vision of a better possibility and the good feelings it brings energizes you even more to follow through. Once you know about Unique Ability, it's almost impossible not to feel its pull.

  The flip side of this is that *not* using your Unique Ability can feel even more confining and frustrating once you know the difference. This is something you can use to your advantage, as we'll discuss shortly.

- **Unique Ability seeks and attracts Unique Ability.** People who are passionate and talented immediately recognize and want to work with others who are also passionate and talented. Once you focus on your own Unique Ability, you start to notice Unique Ability in others too, especially those that complement yours. There are so many examples of Unique Ability in action in the world—not just in high-profile people like sports stars, entertainers, great artists, entrepreneurs, and esteemed leaders, but also in countless examples of "ordinary" people who elevate what might be thought of as everyday tasks and activities to ingenious and often inspiring new heights. Once you start to see it more clearly, you can tap into this abundance of different forms of genius and the passion that drives it.

- **Strengths trump "well-roundedness."** Everyone's better off when they focus on their strengths. Doing something that's not your Unique Ability deprives someone with a strength in that area of the opportunity to use it. The desire to be well-rounded at the expense of focusing on Unique Ability is trading the opportunity to achieve genius level at something for the opportunity to develop "a lot of strong weaknesses"—a recipe for mediocrity. The Unique Ability mindset gives you permission, once and for all, to confidently focus on what you love and are best at. For some, this is a major change in perspective.

- **Teamwork rules.** No matter how great you are as an individual, you can accomplish more by collaborating with others who have talents and passions that complement your own. Teamwork is the key to unlocking the potential to achieve whatever you want. A team of people, each working in their Unique Ability and focusing together on a common goal, can tap into energies that no single individual could ever hope to embody. In fact, teamwork is the central skill set that allows you to fully unlock the power of Unique Ability, yours and others'. Teamwork is such a large and important topic, and we've learned so much about it over the past 20 years, that we decided to dedicate another entire book in this series to this fundamental ability and how to maximize it in every area of your life.

- **Unique Ability is a frustration filter.** Choosing to invest your time and energy in relationships and situations that support and utilize Unique Ability eliminates a lot of frustration and wasted time, making life easier and more enjoyable.

A special tool: WinStreak®.
Here's a very simple and powerful little exercise you can do if you have a smart phone or tablet. It will have a profound impact on your confidence and thinking as you begin to expand your understanding and consciousness of Unique Ability. Download WinStreak, the free app from Strategic Coach, available for iOS or Android. You can record "wins" and track them daily or as often as you choose.

Open the app and for today's date, enter a minimum of three achievements or "wins" that have happened as a result of reading this book. They could include new things you've realized, changes you've made, steps of the process you've completed—anything you see as progress on your Unique Ability. Repeat this at regular intervals. Weekly is a good place to start unless you're making progress so quickly you'd rather do it more often.

Seeing your progress from one WinStreak session to the next helps keep you focused on what you're gaining and measures your progress based on where you've come from, rather than by the ideal of where you'd like to be. Like the horizon, that ideal is ever-advancing as you move toward it. It's great to provide a sense of direction, but not great for measuring against because it sets up a game you can never win.

The challenge to change.
As we mentioned earlier, one potential hazard of being excited and energized to do more of your Unique Ability is that it can

also shine a light on everything that's not your Unique Ability and causes you pain and frustration.

Once you see your Unique Ability clearly and understand what it feels like to use it and be valued for it, it can be pretty hard to maintain any enthusiasm for doing anything else. And yet, until you figure out how to get to this new "normal" where you're spending a lot more time in your Unique Ability, the gap between what's true and what's possible can be an irksome source of discontent. Fortunately, it's like the grain of sand in the oyster that becomes the beginning of a pearl. The irritation can be what prompts the transformation of some very basic raw material (your everyday activities and choices) into something precious (happiness, freedom, and an ability to generate all the rewards, financial and otherwise, you want and need).

The best way to counter these sorts of feelings is to spring into action quickly. Take any step to start focusing more on your Unique Ability and you'll begin to see encouraging results that make further progress easier. Feel free to start in a small way if that's what feels most comfortable. It doesn't matter if you go fast or slow. The important thing is to take action. Then you can review the results—the WinStreak app we mentioned is a great way to do this—and figure out what to do next. If it doesn't work, at least you'll learn that and know to try something else. This counts as progress!

The extra rewards.

The work you do in setting yourself up to succeed in the biggest possible way with your Unique Ability has many rewards. Of course there's the way you feel when you get to do more of what you love and see it produce great value for others. And there are the particular rewards you've identified that have kept you doing all the work to get to this point in the book. Here are a couple of others you may not have thought of to add to that list:

- **No competition.**
  When you're being your best self, you're using your Unique Ability. Your Unique Ability describes exactly what you need to do to win in life, and because it's unique, there's no competition. You're the world's foremost expert in your Unique Ability. It's yours, and yours alone, so why not see how far you can take it?

- **Centered and in control.**
  Unique Ability clarity puts you right in the center of your life, and in control. Once you have 100 percent clarity on what you bring to the table, and why you do the things you do, there's much less chance of you getting swayed by what others want you to do. You could do any number of things, with lots of different kinds of people, with a variety of results, but only a few of those will develop your Unique Ability.

  A by-product of talent and success is that people will often ask things of you. You'll be faced with a variety of opportunities, some of which may be flattering or prestigious, so the more clear and confident you are about your Unique Ability, the more likely you are to make the best choice for your own future. You'll avoid messes associated with doing things that are not your Unique Ability.

  For many people, it's still a process to learn how to say no. You have more freedom. You're grounded and centered in your own self, and you can decide with clear criteria which opportunities and relationships to say yes to, and which to avoid. The more you do this, the easier it gets.

Exercise

5 Quick Unique Ability® Strategies

"Your eyes only see and your ears only hear what your brain is looking for."

Dan Sullivan

What can I do with my "You On A Page"?
You have a new awareness and appreciation of your Unique Ability—and words to describe it. So, what now?

You've given your brain information that will help you see the world in a new way. Maybe you're looking back to the past and thinking, "Oh, that's why such and such didn't work out." If a situation didn't use your Unique Ability or a person didn't appreciate it, there was likely some stress and a lack of confidence. Or, you might be thinking, "That's why that was so easy" and looking to the future wondering, "How can I do more of this?"

Here we want to get you started with some simple strategies. Let's look at five ways to use your Unique Ability even more!

What To Do With "You On A Page"

1. **Keep it visible.** Type it up and keep it on your desk, post it on your wall in your office, put it on your fridge, or keep it inside a notebook or wallet that you carry with you all the time. Keep it visible as a daily reminder of your "zone" where you're the most confident and creative. Create a small card that you can carry around with you and pull it out to remind yourself of the value you create for others.

2. **Share it.** Share it with your family, the team you work with, those who care about you, and those who answered your Unique Ability Question.

3. **Find a new way to use it.** How can you use it more at work? Are you using it at home with your family? What types of activities would really make great use of your talents and driving passion? What kind of people would really benefit? Brainstorm ways to create even more value using your Unique Ability.

4. **Use it as a filter.** Whether you're looking at taking on new responsibilities, looking for new relationships, looking for a new job, or searching out new activities to engage in, use it to help you assess whether the new opportunity uses your Unique Ability and allows you to do what you love to do and do best. Run through your Best Habits and see if you are free to be yourself.

5. **Help someone else.** Reinforce other people's strengths and help them figure out what they do best and love doing. Suggest that they send out The Unique Ability Question, do their Kolbe, or complete their CliftonStrengths profile to help them get clear as well.

Many people have called their Unique Ability their touchstone, their pole star, or their North Star. It reminds you how not to get lost and how to be your best self.

Opening up opportunities.
Your Unique Ability, however precisely you've been able to define it so far, gives you a way to quickly and concisely articulate what you're naturally good at to other people. Once others understand it, they can help you find opportunities to use it more, and they can tap into it even more themselves. "Packaging" it, as we've done here by putting it into specific words, makes it easier to remember, and repeat or promote. This makes it more likely that you'll be remembered or recommended when others need someone with your talent and passion.

Giving others direction.
Clearly articulating what you love to do so others can understand it will also increase the likelihood that when opportunities are sent your way, they'll be things you'll actually want to do. This is preferable to someone sending you things they thought you'd be good at but that *you're* not really that excited about. Often, the only way people know what lies behind the results they identify with your Unique Ability is when you tell them. Giving them this information provides them with valuable direction about how to engage your passion for your benefit and theirs.

For example, someone might say, "You're a great cook, and whatever you make is always different and delicious." Perhaps you love finding new recipes and have a skill for sourcing really good ones and executing them superbly. On the other hand, maybe you're an innovator who has an innate understanding of ingredients and the basic principles of cooking, and loves to create brilliant dishes in the moment without using recipes at all.

In the first case, you might love a gift of the hottest new cookbook, or be thrilled to help when someone is planning a dinner party and having difficulty figuring out the menu. However, if you're the improviser who never uses a recipe, you may not really appreciate the cookbook, and the dinner party queries could stress you out. What might really get you excited, though, is a friend calling you in a panic because they have nothing in their pantry but tinned fish, beans, and some condiments, and they need to make something edible for unexpected guests—exactly what would stress out the great recipe-finder!

Grow your Unique Ability resource pool.
Sharing your Unique Ability will make it easier to keep your project of pursuing it alive and moving forward. Another by-product is the excitement and enthusiasm you spark in others. Unique Ability is a concept with a strong emotional pull. Those who hear about it tend to be eager to learn more and are naturally curious about what theirs might be. If you help someone else discover their Unique Ability, you'll benefit not only from assisting them, but from getting clearer about their Unique Ability and how it might be useful to you or others you know.

A touchstone for life.
Many people have called their Unique Ability their touchstone, their pole star, or their North Star. It reminds you how not to get lost and how to be your best self. Once you've become more conscious of your Unique Ability and put words around it, you'll have it for life. It will keep improving and expanding, but it will always be with you.

Notebook Exercise: 5 Quick Unique Ability Strategies

In your Notebook, come up with one action item for each of the five strategies in the chart. It's very powerful to have your newfound awareness, and it's a whole other level to do something with it.

5 Quick Unique Ability® Strategies

1. Keep it visible. What are you going to do to keep yours top of mind? By when will you do it?

First Action	By When
Post my Unique Ability by my computer and carry it with me. Look at it daily.	Starting Monday

2. Share it. Who else would you like to share it with? By when? We suggest sharing it first with those people who responded to the Unique Ability Question. Or, show it to your spouse or kids to see what they think.

First Action	By When
Send it to the people who answered my UA Question and get their feedback. Show to my family.	Tomorrow

3. Find a new way to use it. What's one way you know you could use it more, starting right now, in any area of your life?

First Action	By When
Talk to my wife about my vision for our vacation property and get her excited about the possibilities.	Date night next week

4. Use it as a filter. What's one new opportunity for the future where you can use it to assess whether it's a good fit?

First Action	By When
Look at prospect list and make sure they align with my Unique Ability.	Two weeks Friday

"I keep a little summary card of my Unique Ability in my wallet, and every once in a while when I'm sifting through it, I reread it. I also keep a copy on my bulletin board, so sometimes I look over at it and think, 'Well, let's just remind myself of what I do.' I like how it's summarized in the ten points. I can't say I've memorized all ten, but it really strings it together with the one statement."

Ben Stellino

"I keep a printout on top of my desk, so every day, I'm looking down and I'm just reinforcing about where I should be spending my time. What I realized, and it's not rocket science, is that when I'm actually able to live in my Unique Ability and do things according to my Best Habits, I have so much more confidence. My stress level's lower. The work I can do is better. When I'm feeling less productive, or I'm not really feeling in sync, or I have a lack of confidence, I usually find that it's because I've steered away from those things. So by looking at my Unique Ability, I can bring myself back in and regain my confidence."

Pamela Kan

"Identifying my Unique Ability took my relationship with my wife to a whole new level because one of the things that came out is that my wife is always spot on. She doesn't offer up advice to me usually, but when she does, she has historically always been right. I realized that I needed to open up to that because a key part of my Unique Ability is 'quickly cutting to the core' for everyone else, but I used to think, 'I don't need anyone to do that for me.' It was kind of like my mantra. But just because I'm doing it for others doesn't mean I can coach myself. My wife has been the voice I go to, and she's been very, very helpful. I would never have allowed someone so close to me to coach me before going through The Unique Ability Discovery Process."

Scott Cohen

"Having the language around your Unique Ability certainly supports you to have greater intentionality because intention is a consciousness around action. It also becomes a filter for me in life for what I will and won't say yes to, or how I might operate. As you grow in your leadership and there's more demand for it in the world, it becomes really important where you're going to place it. I have found that the confidence to say yes or no or to align opportunities with Unique Ability is a crucial awareness to develop."

Adrienne Duffy

"After going through the process, I came up with a 'reality check' to keep me focused on my Unique Ability. Before taking on any new activity, I ask myself four questions: 1. Could someone else do this? 2. Am I doing this out of fear? 3. Is this activity going to help me get to my bigger future? 4. If I could only get three things done today, would this be one of them?"

Daryl Braham

THE BOTTOM LINE:

- The world looks different through a Unique Ability lens—you now have a new-found awareness.
- Unique Ability Teamwork is a crucial next step.
- Use the WinStreak app to keep track of your progress and keep your confidence high.
- With Unique Ability, there's no competition, and you're centered and more in control of your life.
- Start putting your Unique Ability to use right away.

The End ...
... And The
Beginning ...

Unique Ability®
2.0

The End ...
And The Beginning ...

So now that you're in the driver's seat, let's see what the open road looks like. The work you've done in this book and the Notebook, and the insights you've gained about yourself in the process, will change your future for the better, and that's no small thing. One of the thinking contexts Dan Sullivan likes to give to our clients is the notion that "everything you've done up to now is just the beginning"—let's call it Game One. It was all just preparation for what you're about to do now and in your much bigger future: Game Two. This is a game you're set up to win.

One of the hardest things about writing this book was knowing where to end it, and that's because understanding your Unique Ability truly is a gateway. We're very excited that you've taken this step—and for all the doors it can open in your life and the new possibilities that will bring. We also know that there are new skills and knowledge that will help you apply it and get the most out of it along the way. Many of these go beyond the scope of this book, which is why we decided, ten years after writing our first book on Unique Ability, to make this a series: *Unique Ability 2.0*.

If you think back to Chad's story at the beginning of the book, there was a point at which he came to us at Strategic Coach, when his considerable natural talents and experience that had brought him so far were not enough to get him through the next set of obstacles. That's common. People often stumble upon us or seek us out when they know they need something extra to break through to the next level.

In your case, you may have picked up this book because something in its subject matter resonated with a need you felt or a commitment you'd made to yourself to courageously move forward, go deeper, discover more about yourself in order to live a more satisfying life, and give more of your best creative self to the world. Or perhaps someone gave it to you hoping that's what you would do with it. Now that you understand and can articulate your Unique Ability better, you're poised to be able to do just that. Perhaps you've already started.

What's next?

Wherever you're at, there is one skill set that will multiply your efforts many times over if you can master it, and that's teamwork—specifically, Unique Ability Teamwork, the skill of being able to get Unique Abilities working together around a common purpose. The next book in this series, *Unique Ability 2.0: Team,* will go deep on this subject, drawing on our many years of experience with entrepreneurial teams and also with teamwork at home, in our communities, and in all our key relationships. Once you begin to recognize it, you'll see there's a place for Unique Ability Teamwork everywhere you collaborate with others.

If you're ready to use your Unique Ability to make a much bigger impact out in the world, whether it's in business, community work, the arts, sports, recreation, or any other form of activity, this next book is for you. We simply couldn't squeeze everything into the book you have in your hands. Doing the work in this first book is like putting on your own oxygen mask first on an airplane. *Unique Ability 2.0: Team* is about what you do after that—being a hero to the people who matter most to you and contributing your unique talents in ways where the whole becomes greater than the sum of its parts. It's through teamwork that you get to realize the sense of great abundance that comes with harnessing passion and purpose, and directing it to a common goal.

Shannon Waller, our resident Entrepreneurial Team Strategist and lead Team Program coach, has made Unique Ability Teamwork the focus of her life's work. In *Unique Ability 2.0: Team*, you'll get the benefit of her tremendous insight, voracious reading on the subject, and learning and experience with thousands of team members and entrepreneurs over the past 20 years. And Shannon's not all business. She's just as curious and willing to experiment in applying teamwork principles at home, with her family, and everyone who helps to make their busy lifestyle work, and to bring this wisdom as one of the gifts she offers in her personal relationships as well.

Once you've got a great handle on your Unique Ability, begun to see Unique Ability in others, and figured out the basics of teamwork, you'll have multiplied your ability to design the life you want and to create anything you're passionate about, with the help of others and their Unique Abilities. This is what makes it possible to tap into human potential, and what drives us on the deepest level, to draw the right people together and align their visions, energies, talents, and resources to create remarkable things. The greatest accomplishments of humankind have all had Unique Ability Teamwork at their core, even if it wasn't conscious. When it's done consciously, the confidence and acknowledgement this gives to everyone involved is truly what "dream teams" and dream partnerships are made of.

You'll be hearing more from us.
Since each of our Unique Abilities (which we've shared in Appendix C) drives us to develop and deepen the concept and application of Unique Ability, you'll be hearing more from us. We're always learning more, and we'll keep sharing. With the basics in hand, as you build your bespoke life, you may find yourself going over this material again and again. There's a lot here—much too much to squeeze out all the value on the first pass—so enjoy the insights that come as you go over the exercises or read the text again with eyes fresh from your own new experience of your Unique Ability in action. We've said earlier that your Unique Ability evolves, though you at the core remain you. You might say you become even *more* you, or a more focused, purposeful version of you, where more of your uniqueness gets to be expressed and creates even more value for everyone around you.

In the meantime, welcome to Game Two: the rest of your life! We celebrate and salute your Unique Ability. Here's to all you've done and will continue to do to bring its particular combination of usefulness and magic to the world in ever-increasing ways.

If you'd care to share, we'd love to hear your story as it unfolds. Come visit us at **uniqueability.com** to connect with our Unique Ability community and continue the conversation.

Until next time ...

Appendices

Unique Ability®
2.0

Appendix A
Recommended Resources

These resources all have a Unique Ability theme, and some may be useful to help you see different facets of your Unique Ability or how central it is to designing a successful life. It is by no means a comprehensive list, but if you're looking to better understand aspects of your Unique Ability, these are a few of the sources we most often find ourselves recommending and quoting. Unless otherwise noted, these are books.

Kolbe

Conative Connection: Acting on Instincts. By Kathy Kolbe. (Kolbe, 1990; available at kolbe.com)

Powered By Instinct: 5 Rules for Trusting Your Guts. By Kathy Kolbe. (Kolbe, 2003; available at kolbe.com)

Delve deeper into the meaning and uses of your Kolbe A Index results with these books that focus on why we do what we do, and how to use this knowledge to create a better life. *Conative Connection* focuses more on the entire Kolbe system, with an overview on how it works and how to use it. *Powered By Instinct* provides rules for working with your particular strengths.

Kolbe also offers a host of useful audios in their online store at kolbe.com, and on audible.com. The Natural Advantage audio that matches your results may give you deeper insight into how you operate. Contact Kolbe if you're unsure which one applies to you.

And, for younger people, **the Kolbe Y Index for Youth** is an alternative assessment to the Kolbe A Index. It is suitable for those with a 4th grade reading level to seventeen years of age. It's available at kolbe.com under "Assessments."

CliftonStrengths

StrengthsFinder 2.0. By Tom Rath. (Gallup Press, 1st ed. 2007)

If you've done the CliftonStrengths assessment as part of The Naming Path, you may have already purchased and read this book.

For more on how to leverage your strengths and the strengths of others, we also often recommend:

Strengths Based Leadership: Great Leaders, Teams, and Why People Follow. By Tom Rath and Barry Conchie. (Gallup Press, 2008)

Other Resources

The Great Work of Your Life: A Guide for the Journey to Your True Calling. By Stephen Cope. (2012)

In this book, Stephen Cope explores what we call Unique Ability through the eyes of yogis with the guidance of the *Bhagavad Gita*. He uses the stories of well-known visionaries as diverse as Jane Goodall, Ludwig van Beethoven, Mohandas

Ghandi, and Robert Frost, intertwined with stories of ordinary people, to illustrate that finding and focusing on one's unique calling requires courage, perseverance, and killing off the alternatives.

If you're feeling at all challenged by what your Unique Ability calls you to do in your life, this book will help you see that you're in great company. You might also see that by going through The Unique Ability Discovery Process, you have a significant advantage over others throughout history who have had to make their way along the path without it. Either way, it makes a wonderful companion to working your own way through the process.

The Talent Code: Greatness Isn't Born. It's Grown. Here's How. By Daniel Coyle. (2009)

How do you make the most of your innate talents? Daniel Coyle offers three practical strategies to grow your talent by working with the physiology of your brain, based on neurological studies and firsthand research with some of the world's most talented people.

Outliers: The Story of Success. By Malcolm Gladwell. (2008)

Malcolm Gladwell often writes about aspects of genius. This book, by illuminating the seemingly random and unique circumstances that may explain why some groups of people become extraordinarily good at certain things, helps bring home the importance and potential of consciously cultivating talent when we see it. From the perspective of Unique Ability, his case studies leave one with the sense that the right support structure (even if it appears by chance) is vital to the development of talent. It's great motivation to identify and optimize the circumstances that support your Unique Ability, or that of those around you, to maximize its impact on the world.

And, just for fun:

The Rosie Project: A Novel. By Graeme Simsion. (2014)

This whimsical best-selling novel can be read as a charming and humorously inventive love story, but it's also a delightful reminder of how, by stepping out of your comfort zone once in a while, you may find uses for your Unique Ability you never imagined that bring very different and desirable kinds of rewards.

On The Night You Were Born. By Nancy Tillman. (2010)

This much-loved children's book celebrates the uniqueness of a newborn. In each of her books, Nancy Tillman beautifully conveys her message to all children that they are loved, and that they each have innate, immeasurable value.

The video of **Jim Carrey's commencement address at the Maharishi University of Management** is available in its entirety at the time of this printing on YouTube. A Google search for "Jim Carrey Maharishi" should find it for you.

Appendix B

Five Unique Ability Examples

Seeing someone's well-crafted Unique Ability Statement and 10 Best Unique Ability Habits may be the closest you ever get to being inside the head and heart of another human being. Though yours will obviously be completely unique to you, when you're working toward your own, it sometimes helps to get some inspiration by looking at what others have done. Here are some examples from real people who have gone through the entire Unique Ability Discovery Process.

Reading through them may give you some ideas about how to express your own uniqueness, how deep to go, or what your own version might look like. Some of these people are well-described in the book, like Chad Johnson, and others you won't know anything about. Notice what you can tell about them just from reading their full Unique Ability descriptions.

Chad Johnson CEO & Chief Inspiration Officer
Dufur, Oregon
Kolbe: 5 2 9 3
CliftonStrengths: Woo, Positivity, Futuristic, Maximizer, Communication

My Unique Ability is being the real Chad, living life like it's a crazy, fun adventure movie, and inspiring and equipping people to take risks so they can experience richness in the areas that matter most and live their lives with more passion and delight.

Chad's 10 Best Habits

1. **Create memorable unique experiences.** I spontaneously and deliberately create unique experiences that bring people together, add value, make the average or ordinary more enjoyable, and create memories that people will always treasure. I engage them in playing a fun game that results in an environment that elevates them and helps them see life from a more positive perspective. This adds color, joy, and delight to their lives and creates a "wow" factor.

2. **Engage people.** I believe that you can have everything you want in life if you help enough other people get what they want. When I'm passionate about something and strongly desire a certain outcome, I'm fanatical, tenacious, and creative about getting what I want. I research and ask tons of questions to create a war chest of data and information to find out what other people want. Then I immerse myself in it so it becomes part of who I am and map out a dynamic, evolving master plan of how I'll go about bringing people to a desired outcome or decision and get them what they want. I set things up so that I can't help but win others over and create a win-win solution.

3. **Anchored in my faith.** My relationship with Jesus Christ is at the epicenter of who I am. I feel a deep sense of gratitude for the gift of salvation and the freedom that comes from that. I believe I'm put here to use my God-given gifts for His plans and purposes, and I have a huge awareness that it's not about me. I truly believe in a loving, benevolent God who protects and cares for me, and I want others to experience that in all areas of their lives. This faith frees me up to live an abundant life and to bless others and be blessed by others.

4. **Positive future.** I have a vision of a future that's amazing. I know that what I've pictured in my mind is going to happen. I patiently wait for the right time for things to unfold and am always building strong foundations that will make the future possible.

5. **Live the adventure.** I see life as a grand adventure, a romantic drama, an action-packed thriller, and a comedy all at once. I live life as a movie that I want to watch with my children and grandchildren. I live life differently, experiment, adapt, and play. I engage in new, big, or physical challenges in order to really feel alive, to reduce stress, to improve my health, to light me up, and to inspire others to take risks and have breakthroughs, and more exciting goals and adventures.

6. **Transparent communicator.** I communicate transparently and share myself openly, honestly, freely, and from my heart. I see my own faults clearly and ask for forgiveness when I mess up. I'm always real. This authenticity creates trust and helps people feel safe. It allows them to feel free to drop the façade and be truly genuine, and to 'fess up to their own shortcomings, which is where real progress and healing can take place. This then creates paradigm shifts and breakthroughs in personal relationships that lead people to a bigger, better future in the areas that matter most.

7. **Maximizer.** I play the game to be the best and act as a catalyst to make everything around me better, especially the things that are in line with my "Giant Five."[5] I strive to create balanced success, where we're not maximizing one thing at the expense of another. I plug into existing systems or structures and love taking them to new levels of excellence. I seek out and utilize clean, simple, quality

5 Chad's "Giant Five": 1. Faith 2. Wife, Jenise 3. Children 4. Health 5. Unique Ability/God-given talents

environments that allow me to be fully present and to be my best.

8. **Help people grow.** I see people's passion, interest, and the spark that lights them up. I'm constantly evaluating people and looking to see if they have a desire to grow, and if they do, I coach and equip them with strategies and tools that provide direction, insight, and freedom so they're inspired to do better at whatever they're committed to, and can use their God-given gifts to the fullest of their potential, go forward, get better, see progress, experience joy in their lives, and are elevated to be who they were meant to be.

9. **Inspirational living.** I truly believe that extraordinary things can happen for ordinary people and want others to believe that as well. I want my own life story to be a testimony and source of inspiration to show other people what's possible. I want to be a flame that's lighting other fires. I believe everyone is created special. I greet everyone with a smile, engage with them, thank them, listen to what they're interested in, and connect with them. I want to make their day, to be a bright spot, to entertain them, to help them find renewed faith or relationship, to help them have more fun, to bring joy and delight, and to get a smile out of them.

10. **Relationship rich.** People matter to me. I want to leave behind a legacy of incredibly valued relationships. My marriage, children, and grandchildren will be the scorecard by which my leadership and impact are measured. This is how I define a masterpiece life.

Jean-Pierre Blanchet Private Wealth Management

Financial Planner   Quebec City, Quebec

Kolbe: 5 2 8 6

CliftonStrengths: Arranger, Futuristic, Communication, Relator, Strategic

My Unique Ability is building simple solutions using play and storytelling to connect people to their emotions so they make the right decisions and create the future they really want.

Jean-Pierre's 10 Best Habits

1. **Visionary builder.** I'm confident that I know how to build things. I have an artistic way of seeing the world—I see the harmony in things. When I see the raw material at hand, I have a vision of building something that will have a purpose—of creating a better future or realizing people's rising dreams. I see the vision clearly in my mind, using all of my senses.

2. **Strategic.** I see solutions for people's problems and challenges that will simplify their lives. I adapt to different people's situations and help create new futures for them.

3. **Provoke action.** I provoke, challenge, and push people out of their comfort zones in order to create imbalance and get them to move forward in the right direction. I help them see a new reality, which forces them to change and bring about harmony in their lives. I help people realize that their future is possible and sell them on making it a reality.

4. **Dream team builder.** I see life as something you can build to be a better person. I build roles around people's

strengths that will help them get better, be happy, and develop new capabilities. I foster an entrepreneurial mindset where people are in charge of their own results, and they are their own boss in their area of specialty. I pay attention to them, take care of them, and create fun games to give them personalized gifts so they feel important in my life.

5. **Simplify.** When I see any form of complexity, I perceive the simpler form within seconds and put the complexity into a story that people can understand. This gives people clarity, positivity, and a sense of hope that their future will be better than their past.

6. **Authentic relationship builder.** I'm honest, authentic, and share openly. I kinesthetically feel people's emotions—pain, joy, or sadness. I pinpoint what will make them vibrate, and I feel what they want. It's like I can hear the music of their soul, I can play with it, and I can let them hear it. I listen with an open mind to their stories, ask a few questions, look around for clues to understand them, and quickly get a reading of their lives and connect with them. This connection makes them a friend automatically and builds long-term relationships. I use these clues and understanding as raw materials to build their future with them.

7. **Storyteller.** I tell stories using passion, humour, and emotion, and adjust each story to the realities of the person I'm talking to. I talk about their world, learn their language, and adjust my vocabulary so they can connect to the real thing. I tell a story that they can make their own. As we talk, they add to the story, and we build it together.

8. **Persevere.** I can suffer and endure a lot of psychological and physical pain before letting go. I strive to be the best in my domain by building something healthy, where everyone who touches me gets richer and transforms their life.

9. **Trustworthy.** I'm a man of one word. I never step down from what I'm saying, and I always keep my promise. I never deceive anybody. As a result, people rely on me and trust me.

10. **Play the game of life.** I believe that it's through play that you learn the game of life, so I organize my world as a funny place. I tell jokes and make fun of situations to make people laugh and to keep them off-balance. I get them out of their heads, detach them from their thoughts, connect them with their emotions, and put them into their hearts. I believe that the soul itself is joyful and looks for joy. I make them touch their soul so they experience happiness and joy.

Ginger Price Cosmetic Dentist & Designer Phoenix, Arizona

Kolbe: 2 3 9 4
CliftonStrengths: Strategic, Activator, Achiever, Futuristic, Ideation

My Unique Ability is visualizing creative ideas and designing solutions, magnetically attracting the components to manifest them, and streamlining processes to achieve results as quickly as possible, while making sure everyone has a great time getting there.

Ginger's 10 Best Habits

1. **Achiever.** I'm highly productive; set and drive toward bigger and bigger goals; create tangible, symbolic milestones to reach for that mentally raise my level and inspire me. I get to the result as quickly as possible, blowing through any obstacles that may come up, while making sure everyone has a great time getting there.

2. **Visionary.** When I have new ideas or a vision of what's possible or what could be ideal, I use my intuition, brainstorm, and simplify, which magnetically attracts all of the components necessary to manifest it. Whatever I set my mind to, it shows up!

3. **In motion.** I'm always moving forward, taking action quickly and assuming others will move behind me. I chart the course and set things in motion.

4. **Simplify.** I'm always streamlining any process to refine it to its fewest number of steps in order to reduce stress and more efficiently achieve the goal.

5. **Designer.** I quickly see through the current state to what the potential is, see the patterns, identify what's wrong with the equation, and then visualize three-dimensional solutions in my head. This allows me to free up the space to maximize the spatial flow, unlock the hidden potential, and revamp it so it's functional, practical, and pretty—and creates a relaxed, open, clean, serene, and calming feeling and experience.

6. **Creative.** I seek out variety in order to keep my creativity fresh, get reenergized, stimulate my brain, and trigger

ideas, keeping myself constantly learning and growing. You never know what you're going to discover.

7. **Strategic.** I see things as a fun game and constantly develop strategies. I think and act strategically—all of my actions have a bigger goal.

8. **Positive.** I wake up happy. I'm very conscious of setting the vibe around me, so wherever I am, it's a happy place to be, allowing things to get done easily with no muss, no fuss, while at the same time focusing on the best in each other, and expecting the best.

9. **Woo.** I strategically ask questions to find out what people want; listen with interest, curiosity, patience, and without being attached to the outcome; let them unravel; match where they're going; get them in the problem with me; let them be in charge; try to enlighten them along the way; and then reflect the strategy back to them in a way that wins them over and makes it easier for everyone.

10. **Integrity.** I hold myself and others to a set of high standards. I am generous and go the extra mile, but I draw a line that I won't go beyond, in order to accomplish a tangible outcome that's high-quality and done with a sense of integrity.

Oabona Kgengwenyane Management Consultant

Gaborone, Botswana
Kolbe: 7 4 8 2
CliftonStrengths: Responsibility, Learner, Achiever, Includer, Futuristic

My Unique Ability is looking at the world through a global lens; thriving on new, innovative ideas; being on the top frontier of learning; passionately engaging with people equitably; and coming up with robust solutions that are executed in a disciplined manner in order to generate energy and excitement about the future and create value for society.

Oabona's 10 Best Habits

1. **The responsible leader.** I honor my word; live with trust, integrity, and "botho"; and remain grounded. I treat people with love, respect, and fairness, and acknowledge them as human beings. I believe that in the end, we're all the same—we're all students of life. I take charge and influence followers to move in the right direction, proactively attacking the potential to develop an ego or arrogance, or to take advantage of others.

2. **Big ideas.** I look at the world through a global lens and thrive on new ideas. I readily challenge the status quo, do things differently, offer different perspectives, listen excitedly to other people's perspectives, and innovate new ways of doing things in order to transform whatever I touch into something of improved value.

3. **Big vision.** I envision a picture of society in the future and come back to see what can be done in the now to facilitate that future coming to bear. I create a compelling

picture of the vision and share it with others to generate energy and excitement about the future.

4. **Bold decision maker.** When I see opportunities that are aligned with the bigger vision and are feasible, I make bold decisions and take actions that create value for society.

5. **Analytical thinker.** I research, plan, and prepare. I quickly comprehend scenarios, synthesize, analyze, decipher, and come up with the most robust solutions. I then package them in simple ways so they're easier to understand and execute.

6. **World Cup execution.** I use the vision to create longer-term goals, break them down into smaller actions, and track progress. I move forward with drive, discipline, and tenacity to attain set objectives, leaving no stone unturned.

7. **Avid learner.** I am fascinated by and eager to understand how the world works and strive to be on the top frontier of learning. I constantly read, inquire, seek to gain knowledge, and take lessons from past experiences and from nature for the betterment of society.

8. **Sense of wonderment about the world.** I watch people with a young person's sense of wonderment and fascination. I passionately engage with them, inquire, dig deep, and listen with a lack of judgment, and, as a result, people are able to tap into their talents, become more confident, and have the room to blossom and grow.

9. **Storyteller.** I use images, share personal experiences, tell stories, and package insights in such a way that they link to the local context in order to increase the impact of the message. As a result, people get fascinated, can relate and learn, and are better able to reach their desired objectives.

10. **Excite the spirit.** I sing, laugh, and do whatever I can to create a "wow" factor whenever I interact with people. This gets them to laugh or smile and enjoy the experience so they are more creative, freer, can contribute more to idea generation, and live life in a more fulfilled way.

Nicole Pitcher Support Partner Toronto, Ontario

Kolbe: 8 7 4 2
CliftonStrengths: Harmony, Input, Intellection, Learner, Consistency

My Unique Ability is sharing my insightful self-awareness; being an enthusiastic, open-minded learner; tuning in to people's feelings with genuine compassion and empathy; and creating structures that organize words and information in order to be an expert resource, help people feel supported, and create a sense of positivity, harmony, and balance.

Nicole's 10 Best Habits

1. **Expert.** I research, collect, and organize words and information so there's a flow; make a plan; and then articulate and present it in order to pass on knowledge and be a resource for others.

2. **Enthusiastic learner.** I study something new and contemplate ideas, philosophies, and frameworks in order to keep my brain active, provide balance, lighten and shift my thinking, and gain new perspectives that allow me to be more optimistic and bring positivity to people.

3. **Open-minded explorer.** I seek out new and varied experiences, people, and cultures in order to gather new insight, maintain an open mind, and expand my knowledge of how people and the world work.

4. **Cautiously optimistic.** I come prepared for any type of situation and rely on research or experience to make well-informed decisions so I feel safe and can trust the risks I take.

5. **Insightful self-awareness.** I capture my feelings, thoughts, and experiences in writing in order to self-reflect, know myself better, and grow.

6. **Supportive.** I tune in to people's feelings, listen with genuine compassion and empathy, and share perspectives in order to support the people I care about and help them become the best versions of themselves.

7. **Peacekeeper.** I see the areas of agreement and focus people on them and use humour in order to avoid or resolve conflict and create a sense of harmony and balance.

8. **Consistent fairness.** I consistently follow and enforce the rules to make sure there's an equal playing field that ensures fairness.

9. **Organizational ninja.** I follow routines and established procedures, modify them to make them more efficient if necessary, and create structures that help people feel supported and organized.

10. **Resilience.** I create long-term goals, adapt around obstacles, and persist to achieve a final result, or at least have a valuable experience where I gain insight.

Appendix C

About The Authors

This book is an example of Unique Ability Teamwork in action. Each of the authors, along with a huge team of others, brought their own unique talents and passions to this project. We've shared our Unique Abilities here so you can get a sense of how and why we poured our hearts into *Unique Ability 2.0: Discovery*.

Julia Waller

Unique Ability Specialist & Coach

When Julia was about six years old, one of the most meaningful clues to her Unique Ability was already evident, but she would only realize her talents were factory-installed much, much later in life. When a little girl down the street came home with an "unhappy face" sticker on her schoolwork, Julia immediately jumped in to help her. Though she didn't know it then, her life as an educator had begun.

Teaching in Canada, Hong Kong, and Mexico, her personal mandate was to create a safe learning environment where kids could express themselves and become more capable. She loved identifying their talents, and helping develop their potential.

Arriving at Strategic Coach in 1997, she found an entrepreneurial culture that was a much better fit for her desire for autonomy. She learned about Unique Ability, which immediately resonated. Julia was given "permission" to be her best self and was valued for her uniqueness. As a result, she quickly started to find new ways to apply her natural talents. "Everything starts with my passion for making meaningful connections," Julia says. "I love being at the hub of everything and making sure everyone's connected—integrating things that weren't previously integrated."

As a Team Leader in charge of coach training and development, she wanted to make sure her team members had a career path, so she created a process using existing Strategic Coach Program exercises. This turned out to be the fledgling Unique Ability Discovery Process in this book. "Unique Ability is the ultimate systems maximizer. I'm a maximizer at heart. In everything I do, I'm always trying to help people and systems be the best they can be."

Soon, word spread, and other team members asked Julia to guide them through the process too, meeting with her at the local coffee shop. It took a persistent client who understood the value of knowing his Unique Ability and wanted one-on-one coaching that led to more and more Strategic Coach entrepreneurs enrolling in Julia's one-day coaching session. This is how she now happily spends much of her time, while also collaborating to strengthen the company's culture and keeping the team connected and growing.

As mom to Vivienne, she's also passionate about identifying her daughter's talents and creating a safe space for her to become more capable and be her best. Even Julia's chronicling of Vivi's life by capturing meaningful family memories with her camera and in her online journal is a reflection of her natural documenting and connecting talents.

To Julia, the benefits of defining your Unique Ability and living in a Unique Ability culture are abundant: "You get to do what you love most; you don't have to do the stuff you don't like; and you're surrounded by other self-motivated, happy people. Together, you have fun creating the best possible results."

Julia Waller

Kolbe: 6 8 3 3

CliftonStrengths: Maximizer, Connectedness, Developer, Responsibility, Relator

My Unique Ability is making meaningful connections that integrate the parts of a whole and create a path for people to grow and fully express who they are.

Julia's 10 Best Habits

1. **Connector.** I believe that everything's connected and see both the sameness and the uniqueness in everything. I trust that things happen for a reason or when we're ready for them, and let things unfold as naturally as possible. I connect the dots to integrate the parts of the whole and help people feel included in that whole.

2. **Honest Expression.** I express myself honestly, openly, and authentically. I speak up with passion and conviction when I think something is out of integrity, or doesn't feel "right" or fair to me, or to provide balance. I encourage others to do the same so we can all make things better.

3. **Love Talents.** I see the best in people. I value, respect, enjoy, admire, honour, and deeply appreciate their unique talents; help them connect meaningfully with who they are; and support them in finding ways to maximize their contribution and usefulness.

4. **People Developer.** I believe in people's unlimited potential and am committed to their ongoing growth and development. I create paths to help them grow, develop, and fully express who they are. I help them make improvements so they can be their best selves and work in concert with others.

5. **Educator.** I collect, summarize, document, organize, refine, edit, explain, and share information. I show people how things fit together so they have the bigger context and are equipped and ready to handle whatever comes up. I wordsmith to articulate what's meaningful and important to maximize clarity, understanding, and connection. Whenever I can, I teach people what I know to support them in becoming more capable.

6. **Dig Deep.** I relate to people in a personal way and listen with an open mind to create a safe and trusting space where they can open up, be heard, and feel understood. I dig deeper to get to what's real and true, and to understand what makes them tick.

7. **Generous Heart.** I feel things deeply and am easily touched; sense the feelings of those around me; genuinely care about all living things; share my love and warmth; and take action to nurture and support those around me.

8. **Practical Planner.** I look at the overall context, think through the steps and implications as thoroughly as I can, and create a practical plan in order to be prepared, avoid worst-case scenarios, and create the best possible outcome.

9. **Stable Foundation.** I pull things together and design organized systems and processes to maximize efficiency, consistency, and results; to make things easier; to help things move faster; and to provide a stable foundation for action.

10. **Super Responsible.** I set high standards, commit myself fully, take my responsibilities to heart, focus on what needs to be done, work hard with bulldog determination, am extremely thorough, and continually look for improvements in order to achieve the goal in a way that creates the best possible result and meets everyone's needs. I strive to be a positive, responsible, conscientious role model.

Catherine Nomura

Director of Content & Creative Initiatives

As a passionate and talented chef works with food, Catherine works with ideas and possibilities.

In her mind's eye, she sees the world as a vast and largely unexplored storehouse of intriguing "ingredients" that have the potential to create exceptional results. Ingredients, to Catherine, can include situations, needs, concepts, people, processes, and products and services, among other things. Her passion lies in combining them into inspiring new forms to elegantly satisfy an unmet need.

In 1998, when Catherine joined the team at Strategic Coach in a leadership role, she found that her ability to look from a "bird's eye" perspective gave her the big-picture view that was much needed in the growing company. She calls on this talent to provide direction for the company and to its co-founders, Dan Sullivan and Babs Smith, developing new business opportunities, markets, and products that maximize the value of the company's intellectual capital.

Her Unique Ability Statement includes the notion of a vessel as a set of conceptual parameters that others can create into. "Working with Dan, this might involve pointing out the best, most original, or high-potential ideas from a bunch of new thoughts he bounces off me, and reflecting back to him how they multiply other things he's done or thought," she says. To the outside world, it's helping busy entrepreneurs use Strategic Coach thinking to gain new perspectives and create better businesses and lives.

Another use for her talents is in providing in-house guidance on how to best express the evolving nature of what Strategic Coach does. Whether it's directing writers, shaping a company purpose statement, or helping salespeople or marketers capture the most effective way to describe a new offering, Catherine ties together client stories and comments, Dan's latest thoughts, and observations and perspectives from the team and the outside world, helping others zero in on the most potent version of their message. As a chef demonstrates techniques to bring out the best in all the ingredients and their combination in a new dish, Catherine shows how to put ideas together in new ways so others on the team can create new material along the same lines.

"I am passionately motivated to bring out the latent excellent qualities in things, ideas, people, and even sometimes situations, to make sure the really good stuff that may be hidden amongst everything else gets recognized and hopefully used," she says.

In her own writing, Catherine's Unique Ability is used to bring to life on the page the newest advances in Coach thinking, often setting up the context and importance, as well as driving home the impact and relevance.

Personally, Catherine's fascination with ingredients and possibilities plays out in her passion for cooking. "I have a crazy well-stocked pantry with all kinds of unusual things from around the world. I experiment with the unique qualities of ingredients to understand how they might add that special something that's surprising, delightful, and expands people's notion of what's possible."

Always in search of the unique ingredient that becomes the catalyst for a new experience for her various audiences means life is constantly an extraordinary adventure.

Catherine Nomura

Kolbe: 7 2 7 4

CliftonStrengths: Maximizer, Ideation, Strategic, Activator, Connectedness

My Unique Ability is seeking out and collecting resources, opportunities, and possibilities; recognizing the through line from a higher-level perspective; prioritizing and highlighting what has the most momentum, the greatest potential, and the greatest integrity; and offering a conceptual vessel that people can create into to realize bigger possibilities.

Catherine's 10 Best Habits

1. **Stocking the pantry.** I take stock of the resources, catalogue the features or bits of potential that could be maximized, and keep adding interesting, quality, special, secret, unique, or unusual ingredients to the pantry in order to be able to create something definitive that fulfills a special purpose or meets a need in the moment or when the time is ready, with minimal obstacles and frustrations.

2. **Strategic path.** I investigate the lay of the land, get an understanding of the context, weigh the pros and cons, see the blind alleys and strip them away, and then clearly see the most important thing to focus on—the thread, arc, or through line—that has the most momentum and will draw people in the direction they want to go in order to open the pathway for everything to fall into line and work better.

3. **Tzimtzum.** I create a conceptual vessel into which potential can flow to become real. Out of what is possible, which lies in the future, I create structures in the form of

mind maps, outlines, briefs, examples, prototypes, and sketches, and carve out an inviting space with mind-expanding questions, observations, metaphors, imagery, and stories that help others see the bigger possibility that is already real to me in my mind and move them to create into that space.

4. **The tip of the arrow.** I consider the needs of the audience and find the tip of the arrow—the point from which everything makes sense—so I can prioritize what's going to create the greatest forward motion and break through obstacles most easily.

5. **Planting seeds in fertile soil.** I'm a catalyst to integrate people and ideas with environments that will allow them to thrive, grow, and transform. I want people to let go of their fear and resistance regarding the new and the different so they can experience new possibility in a joyful, revelatory way.

6. **Amplifier.** I feel compelled to do justice to concepts, products, services, people, and experiences that I feel will have tremendous value to others. I champion what I believe in because I want people to appreciate really special and unique people and things for who and what they are, so they pay more attention to them, appreciate them, and ultimately do more with them.

7. **Truth and love.** I recognize, increase the value of, and am grateful for the potential in things, people, and situations, and am brutally honest in separating out and highlighting what's most special or unique when necessary in order to keep people focused on being the best version of themselves.

8. **Get above the maze.** When things are stuck, stagnant, or hit a growth plateau, I instinctively look for the higher-level perspective where I can see solutions and strategies others can't see. I constantly think about the higher level and how to get to it.

9. **The next iteration.** I probe and gather data straight from the source in order to find out if the most important part of the message landed with the desired effect, and use this information strategically to do things better or fill in missing bits as we move forward.

10. **Heat-seeking missile.** Once I've sold people on an idea and have hit a point of no return, I work with tenacious determination to make sure the details get handled in the right way, the pieces get put in the right places, the integrity remains intact, and nothing gets lost so we manifest the vision.

Shannon Waller

Entrepreneurial Team Strategist

What Shannon really loves to do is help people see their bigger future and then figure out a strategy that will get them there.

Her natural talents and passion are almost always applied to the Strategic Coach "Front Stage" in her work with clients, their teams, and their families, or with prospective clients. And whether it's a client phone call with an audience of one, a speech delivered to a roomful of entrepreneurs, or hosting a webinar with hundreds of virtual participants, her energy is always in high gear and highly engaging. Shannon likes to get people moving!

Not long after she started at Strategic Coach in 1991, Shannon realized that a team, specifically a Unique Ability Team, is crucial to an entrepreneur's success, leading her to propose and then design several workshop programs specifically for the teams of Strategic Coach entrepreneurs. These workshops get entrepreneurs and their teams on the same page working toward the same result, and have Unique Ability as their foundation.

She is the ultimate champion of great teamwork, saying, "Unique Ability Teamwork is the best, fastest, easiest way for companies to grow. It's also the best strategy for creating the most productive, profitable, rewarding environment, not to mention the most fun. So why wouldn't you do it?"

Shannon's "why" she does what she does—her passion—is very clear to her: "I love aligning people's thinking with what's real, rather than what they think it should be. What's most important to me is that in the end, they're happy with themselves, maximizing their growth, working as part of a team, and fulfilling their purpose."

In her role on the leadership team led by co-founder Babs Smith, Shannon also helps direct the future of Strategic Coach. Her extensive experience and accumulated wisdom make her Babs's go-to strategic partner in developing the company's growth path. As well, Shannon's intuitive capabilities and skill in "rallying the troops" align well with the purpose of this leadership team—another example of Unique Ability in action.

Outside of work, Shannon's focus is on her family. Here, too, her Unique Ability is reflected in how she intuitively sees the essence of everyday situations that arise in family life, and she is overwhelmingly grateful to have this context in parenting her daughters. She explains, "I have a teenage daughter and an almost-teenage daughter, and they're not always the most communicative. I'm totally using my Unique Ability, finding out what's important to them, figuring out the strategy that will connect with them, and then helping them get where they want to go. Just like what I do at work with clients and team members!" Shannon is overwhelmingly grateful to have a context with which to parent her daughters, to know about Unique Ability and to be able to raise them to understand and appreciate their own strengths.

At home, as at work, Shannon pays attention to the people around her and cares deeply. Her Unique Ability sheds light on how she naturally does things when she's at her best and acts as a touchstone she can count on in every area of life.

Shannon Waller

Kolbe: 3 2 9 5

CliftonStrengths: Maximizer, Strategic, Individualization, Arranger, Relator

My Unique Ability is intuitively perceiving the essence of a situation, then innovating and compassionately communicating practical strategies to align people's thinking with what's real so they're happy with themselves, maximizing their growth, working as a team, and fulfilling their purpose.

Shannon's 10 Best Habits

1. **Achiever.** I intuitively perceive the essence of a situation and discover the strategic path to get people where they want to go, without getting lost in the details.

2. **Innovate & communicate.** I innovate and compassionately communicate practical strategies people can use right away to fulfill their purpose.

3. **Challenge assumptions.** I challenge people's unconscious assumptions so they can align their thinking with what's real; make better, more grounded decisions; and reach higher levels of cooperation, collaboration, and teamwork.

4. **Care deeply.** I care deeply about people and accept them for who they are in a nonjudgmental way.

5. **Enthusiastically appreciate.** I enthusiastically help people understand and appreciate their unique capabilities by reflecting their talents back to them so they're happy with themselves and maximizing their contribution to others.

6. **Confidence in growth.** I have confidence in each individual's ability to make progress and am open to people's transformation.

7. **Take action.** I take action to get things and people moving.

8. **Personalize.** I personalize my communication to create maximum impact and relationship.

9. **Adapt & experiment.** I willingly adapt, and experiment with new ideas and approaches.

10. **Align on values.** I operate from and create community with people who are in alignment with my core values.

About Strategic Coach

Unique Ability and Unique Ability Teamwork are at the heart of The Strategic Coach Program for successful entrepreneurs.

Entrepreneurs in Strategic Coach identify their Unique Ability, and then free themselves up to focus on and leverage it as the means to achieve their biggest personal and business goals. A business based on the principles of Unique Ability can be both self-managing and self-multiplying, which gives the entrepreneur increasing freedom, opportunity, and enjoyment. The Strategic Coach Program provides the tools, structure, and thinking space to create an extraordinary entrepreneurial business and quality of life, with the entrepreneur's Unique Ability at its center. The year 2014 marked the 25th anniversary of the first Strategic Coach workshop.

As an organization, Strategic Coach was created by entrepreneurs, for entrepreneurs, and this is reflected in everything it does. The company operates using the same philosophy, tools, and concepts taught in The Strategic Coach Program. With over 100 entrepreneurially-minded team members and four offices—one in Toronto, one in Chicago, one in Los Angeles, and one in the UK—the company continues to grow and enrich its offerings to an expanding global client base. Currently, over 3,000 successful and highly motivated entrepreneurs from over 60 industries and a dozen countries attend Strategic Coach workshops on a quarterly basis.

If you would like more information about Strategic Coach, its programs for entrepreneurs, or its many products for entrepreneurial thinkers, please call **416.531.7399** or **1.800.387.3206**. Or visit **strategiccoach.com.**